WICCACRAFT

PAGAN WITCHCRAFT FOR THE SOLITARY WITCH

SECOND EDITION

LIAM PETER KEENE

Copyright © 2021, 2025 Liam Peter Keene

First published in 2021 by Liam Peter Keene
Second edition published in 2025 by Liam Peter Keene
Norwich, Norfolk, England, United Kingdom.

All rights reserved. No part of this publication may be reproduced, stored or transmitted in any form or by any means, electronic, mechanical, photocopying, recording, scanning or otherwise, without prior written permission from the publisher. It is illegal to copy this book, post it to a website or distribute it by any other means without permission.

Liam Peter Keene asserts the moral right to be identified as the author of this work.

First edition ISBN (Paperback): 978-1-3999-0156-7
Second edition ISBN (Paperback): 978-1-0369-3222-0
Second edition ISBN (eBook): 978-1-0369-3224-4

Note by the Author on the Second Edition

This second edition has been revised and expanded from the first. It now includes new material on the practice of *Goeteia* in Ancient Greece, as well as expanded discussions of *Wiccecræft* among the Anglo-Saxons and the practice of *Seiðr* in Old Norse culture. These sections incorporate historical, literary and archaeological evidence, along with references to authoritative scholarship. The theological and historical chapters have been restructured for clarity, with additional explanations and cross-cultural comparisons to deepen the reader's understanding. The language has been re-edited for precision, consistency and readability, while the formatting and presentation have been updated throughout.

I dedicate this book to the God and Goddess, the Lord and Lady, the Old Gods and to anyone who has been called to the path of Witchcraft

Introduction	1
The History and Etymology of Witchcraft	5
The Indo-European Pagans	5
The Origins of the Pagan Anglo-Saxons	6
Wicca and *Wicce* - The Witch as Diviner and Medium in Anglo-Saxon England	6
The *Vitkar* and *Volur* - Seers and Mediums of the Norse People	12
Witchcraft, *Seiðr* and Homosexuality	15
The *Goetes* and *Manteis* - Ancient Greek Ecstatic Mediums Of The Gods	15
A Summary of the History and Terminology of Witchcraft in Pre-Christian Pagan Europe	21
The Denigration of Witchcraft	22
The Emergence of Modern Witchcraft and Neopaganism	25
The Theology of Wiccacraft	29
The Differences Between Witchcraft and Shamanism	29
The God and Goddess	30
The Calling to be a Witch - Self-Initiation or Coven Initiation	35
Divination and Magic	37
Offerings and Divine Reciprocity	39
The Spirit Realm	41

Symbols of Wiccacraft	41
The Pentagram	41
The Triple Moon	42
The Triskelion	42
Ritual Items and Tools	45
The Historical use of tools in pagan witchcraft	45
Altar	46
Deity Candles	47
Symbols of the God and Goddess	48
Wand	49
Incense and Incense Holder	50
Water Bowl	50
Salt Bowl	51
Offering Bowl	51
Chalice	52
Silk Cord	52
Tealight Candles	53
Anointing Oil	53
Cauldron	55
Runes	55
Crystals	55
Book of Rituals, Ceremonies and Divination	56
Ritual Clothing	56

Symbolic Jewellery	57
Cleansing Bath Ritual	59
Blessing Your Tools	61
Praying to the God and Goddess	63
The Sacred Circle	65
Casting The Circle	65
Closing the circle	68
The First Initiation	71
The Offering Ceremony	75
House Cleansing	79
Moon Ritual	83
The Gods and Goddesses	87
Anglo-Saxon and Norse Pantheon	87
Frey/Ing	87
Freya	88
Frigg	89
Woden/Odin	90
Greek Pantheon	93
Artemis	93
Demeter	94
Dionysus	95
Hecate	97
Persephone	100

Selene	101
Celtic Pantheon	102
Brigid	102
The Dagda	103
Lugh	103
The Eight Seasonal Festivals	105
Yule	107
Imbolc	108
Ostara	110
Beltane/May Day	111
Midsummer/Litha	112
Lughnasa/Lammas	114
Harvest	115
Samhain	116
The Second Initiation	119
Invoking the Gods	133
The Invocation Ritual	134
Evoking the Gods	139
The Evocation Ritual	139
Runes	143
The Runes	144
Divination with Runes	152
Runic Spell	155

Runic Charm	157
Herbal Magic	161
Herbs and other plants that can be used in magical practice	162
Herbal Charm	164
Herbal Cauldron Magic	166
Creating Magical Oil For Spell Work	168
The Third Initiation	173
Conclusion	177
Bibliography	179

Introduction

Wiccacraft is a belief system and practice that is based on those of the Anglo-Saxon diviners and mediums, who were known as *Wiccan* in pre-Christian Pagan England, *Vitkar/Volur* in the Nordic countries and *Goetes/Manteis* in Ancient Greece. The word Wiccacraft is derived from the Old English word *Wiccecræft*, which means "Witchcraft". I have practised Pagan Witchcraft since the year 2000 and I have studied the literary, historical and archaeological sources describing the practice of Pagan Witchcraft in Europe. Wiccacraft is not the same as Gardnerian Wicca, but it does incorporate elements of it into its practices. Wiccacraft emphasises the direct self-initiation of the Witch through the God and Goddess. It views Witchcraft as a calling from the Gods that can be answered through initiation. This book provides three self-initiation rituals for the different stages of your journey on the path of Pagan Witchcraft.

Wiccacraft makes use of invocation and evocation of the Gods, which is a practice that was widespread among the pre-Christian Pagan Witches of Europe. This type of mediumship is described in Ancient Greek, Roman and early Medieval Anglo-Saxon and Norse sources. Through mediumship, you can become one with the Old Gods and experience divine ecstasy, as well as messages in the form of thoughts, feelings or images. The rite of invocation manifests the electrical energy of the Gods in your body, while the rite of evocation enables you to enter the spirit realm.

The Gods and Goddesses called upon in the rituals and ceremonies of this book are from the Anglo-Saxon, Nordic, Greek, Roman and Celtic pantheons. The chapter on Gods and Goddesses provides descriptions of the Gods and Goddesses associated with Witchcraft and the hymns you can use to call upon them. Wiccacraft can be adapted to include the Gods of the pantheons you connect with the most. It is not a path of gatekeeping and it is open to anyone from any background who feels they have a calling to be a Witch, provided that they follow the rule of harming none. Witches are born Witches, but performing self-initiation will help you fully manifest this identity.

Wiccacraft traces the origins of Pagan Witchcraft in Europe to the agricultural/agrarian societies of the Indo-European people. It differs from Shamanism in that Shamanism is rooted in the cultures of hunter-gather societies. Pagan Witchcraft emphasises summoning the Gods, bringing them into one's body and entering the spirit realm, whereas Shamanism is focused mainly on leaving the body to enter the spirit world.

Introduction

In addition to mediumship, divination was another core aspect of the Pagan Witchcraft of Europe. Wiccacraft makes use of runes to assess the past, present and future. Runes are used to interpret the current situation of the person consulting them and the possible future outcome if the querent continues on their current path. If the runes indicate an unfavourable future outcome if the querent makes no changes to their current path, a Witch can throw the runes again to determine if a particular ritual or ceremony will improve the future outcome. Therefore, the runes are a diagnostic tool that can be used to remedy the situation of the person consulting them. This book provides the Witch with methods of throwing and interpreting the runes and lists their meanings.

The eight Pagan seasonal festivals are celebrated in Wiccacraft and this book explains what they symbolise and which Gods are associated with each festival. Each description is accompanied by a hymn, which can be used to incorporate other rituals and ceremonies into your celebration of the seasonal festivals, such as the Offering Ceremony, invocations and evocations and a method of praying to the Gods, all of which are provided in this book.

Wiccacraft makes use of an altar and ritual tools and I have provided techniques of cleansing and blessing these so they can be used in your

WICCACRAFT

Wiccacraftian rites. I have also provided a ritual for casting the sacred circle, which creates a sacred space during rituals and ceremonies. I have included methods of using runes and herbs for magical purposes, which can cause shifts within yourself and help you achieve your goals.

Wiccacraft provides a system for the solitary Witch to fulfil their calling to the path of Pagan Witchcraft so that they can connect with the Gods of the natural world and awaken the divine within themselves.

The History and Etymology of Witchcraft

The Indo-European Pagans

Witchcraft, in the European context, has its origins in the Pagan religions of the first Indo-European people. Witches were religious specialists within a Pagan religious system. They were diviners and mediums who invoked and evoked the Pagan Gods. The Indo-Europeans were agricultural/agrarian people who originated in what is now Ukraine in about 3000 BCE. One group migrated west, further into Europe, while another branch went east into Western Asia. The Indo-European language family is comprised of the Greek, Germanic, Celtic, Italic/Romance/Latin, Balto-Slavic, Albanian, Armenian, Indo-Iranian and the extinct Anatolian, Cimmerian, Dacian, Illyrian, Thracian and Tocharian language families. The descendants of the Indo-Europeans came to make up most linguistic and cultural groups of what is now Europe, Iran and northern India. Many of the Pagan Gods worshipped by people from different Indo-European language families were the same Gods. They would have been known by the same name when the Indo-Europeans constituted one cultural/linguistic group in 3000 BCE, but over time the names changed due to normal linguistic processes.

The Origins of the Pagan Anglo-Saxons

The English language is an Indo-European language in the Germanic family. English is descended from Middle English and Old English. Old English was the language of the Anglo-Saxons, which transformed into Middle English after the invasion of the Norman French in the 11th century. The Anglo-Saxons were an amalgamation of the Germanic Angles, Saxons and Jutes who settled in what is now England in the 5th century. They originated from lands that developed into northern Germany and southern Denmark. The Anglo-Saxons were Pagans when they arrived in Britain. Their pantheon of Gods, beliefs and religious practices were closely related to those of the Norse people (the Norwegian, Swedish, Danish and Icelandic peoples) and of other Indo-European linguistic and cultural groups. The Anglo-Saxon rulers converted to Christianity in the late 7th century. From this historical, cultural and linguistic context, we can trace the origins and meanings of the word "Witch".

Wicca and *Wicce* - The Witch as Diviner and Medium in Anglo-Saxon England

"Witch" is descended from the Middle English word *Wicche*, which referred to both male and female Witches. *Wicche* is, in turn, descended from the Old English words *Wicca* (male Witch) and *Wicce* (female Witch). The plural form of *Wicca* and *Wicce* is *Wiccan*. *Wicca* and *Wicce* are descended from the word *Witega*, meaning "seer" or "one who knows". These terms are related to the Old English word *wigle/wiglian*, which means to "practise divination". All of these words are either descended from or related to the Old English words *wih*, *weoh* and *wig*, which mean "holy" or "sacred". The root of these words is the Proto-Germanic *wihaz*, also meaning "holy". The Proto-Indo European root of all these words is *weyk*, meaning to "separate", which implies something set apart and sacred, in other words "holy". Watkins (1969) has also suggested that the Proto-Germanic root of *Wicca/Wicce* is *Wikkjaz*, meaning "someone who wakes the dead."

The term *Wiccecræft* is the Old English word for Witchcraft and it appears in both legal and ecclesiastical literature from the Anglo-Saxon period. Archaeological finds related to the practice of Wiccecræft have included amulets, burial goods and inscribed charms (Hamerow et al. 2011).

Many other words in Old English are related to *Wicca* and *Wicce*. *Wigol* meant "belonging to divination" (Wood 1914:23). Serjeantson (1936) indicates that witegung means "divination", witegian means "to prophesise" and witig, means "wise". She states that the word *witegung* was used to translate the Latin word *geomantia* (of Greek origin) in an Old English text (Serjeantson 1936). *Geomantia* (geomancy in English) means divination by earth. This translation indicates that one form of divination used by Witches in the Anglo-Saxon Pagan era may have been tossing soil or stones and interpreting the way they landed.

Linguists have had a multitude of theories about the etymology of "Witch" and the debate is still ongoing, despite the clear connections between certain words and their roots that have been discussed above. Liberman (2008) has provided a good summary of the various linguistic theories about the word's etymology that have emerged over the years.

The meaning of all these words, combined with descriptions in Old English texts of *Wiccecræft*, indicate that Witches were religious specialists in divination and mediumship in the pre-Christian Pagan era. They were the "ones who knew", in the sense of knowing divine and sacred wisdom through mediumship and divination. Hall (2007) explains that *Wiccecræft* in Anglo-Saxon England encompassed divinatory and magical practices often linked to healing, protection and social influence, as recorded in legal codes and religious condemnations. Meaney (1981) provides archaeological evidence of amulets and curing stones, indicating that *Wiccecræft* practitioners engaged in material magic alongside spoken charms.

In the Homilies of Aelfric (1881) the connection between a *Wicca/Wicce* and divination is made explicit. Aelfric was an Anglo-Saxon abbot who lived from 955-1010. He states that Witches claim they can diagnose an issue in someone's life through spiritual means (Aelfric 1881). He also writes that Witches' teachings include bringing offerings to stones, trees and wells (Aelfric 1881). The bishop Wulfstan condemned *Wiccecræft* as a Heathen practice (Meaney 2004). These sources clearly show the Pagan nature of Witches in Anglo-Saxon England. In the Laws of King Cnut, there is a paragraph that forbids the Pagan practices of worshipping heathen Gods, the sun, the moon, fire, water, springs, stones, forests, trees and *Wiccecræft* (Serjeantson 1936).

Witches, therefore, played an important role in helping people remain connected to the divinity of nature and the Pagan Gods. In addition to the messages they delivered from the Gods, which they did through divination and mediumship, they knew rituals and ceremonies that would maintain a connection between the community and the divine.

Witches were also involved in the acts of *Gealdor* (spelt Galdor in modern English), an Old English word for spells and charms. Jane Crawford (1963) states that people who used herbs in Anglo-Saxon England used incantations and sang charms over the herbs to ensure their effectiveness. The Old English literature also indicates that Witches performed rituals and ceremonies at crossroads (Crawford 1963). Crossroads were associated with the spirits of the dead. One aspect of Pagan Witchcraft is connecting with the spirit realm to gain knowledge, which is likely why Witches in Anglo-Saxon England performed rituals at the meeting points of roads.

Witchcraft in Anglo-Saxon England was a practice and belief system that emphasised connection with the Gods and spirit realm through mediumship and gaining insight through divination. Divination was not simply a way of looking at a set-in-stone pre-determined future. Whether the Witch were performing divination for themselves or others, it was a means to see what would occur if they stayed on their current trajectory. If the Witch predicted an unfavourable outcome, they would perform rituals and spells to bring stability back to their life and maintain their connection to the divine. Poverty, hardship and instability were seen as being unnatural. Thus divination, ritual and magic were used to overcome these challenges and bring people back to their true path.

THE HISTORY AND ETYMOLOGY OF WITCHCRAFT

The historical, literary, linguistic and archaeological evidence points to the fact that *Wicca* and *Wicce* were specific terms for religious specialists within a Pagan religious system - the seers, diviners and mediums of the Gods and spirits. I, therefore, do not think that the term Witch can be separated from its Pagan origins.

Witchcraft can be described as a religion within a broader Pagan religion. Witches have their own means and practices of connecting with the divine and they perform rituals and ceremonies that are distinct to them. The path of Wiccacraft/Witchcraft is the path of becoming one with the Gods, awakening them from within you and being aware of their presence throughout everything in the natural world. These religious specialists did survive the conversion to Christianity, but they became more secretive and worked primarily as solitary practitioners. Pre-Christian charms/spells have survived and been recorded in post-conversion literature in England, such as Bald's *Leechbook* and the *Lacnunga*, which were composed in the 9th century. There is a charm in the *Lacnunga*, known as the *Nine Herbs Charm*, that invokes the name of the God Woden, the main God of the Anglo-Saxon pantheon. Most charms that survived replace the names of Pagan Gods with those of the Christian God, but the fact that the name Woden continued to be used in the performance of charms and spells indicates that the Pagan element of these rituals persisted.

The *Vitkar* and *Volur* - Seers and Mediums of the Norse People

Wicca and *Wicce* are cognate with the Old Norse words *Vitka* and *Vitki* (the plural is *Vitkar*), both meaning "male Witch". In the *Poetic Edda* (a medieval Icelandic text that contains vast amounts of information about Norse mythology), it is stated that the God Odin practised *Seiðr* with the *Volur* (the singular is *Volva*) in the form of a *Vitka* (Bray 1908). A *Vitka/Vitki* was the male form of a *Volva*. *Volur* were seeresses who practised divination, magic and *Seiðr* in pre-Christian Norse society. *Seiðr*, known as Seid in Modern English, involved invoking and evoking the Gods and spirits, a type of Pagan mediumship. Buchanan (1933) has connected the word *Vitki* (which he translates as a "prophet") and the Old Norse word *vitugr*, meaning "wise", to the Old English words *Witega*, meaning "prophet" and *witig*, meaning "wise". The word *Vitki*, according to Sturtevant (1927), meant "one who is versed and wise" and the word is related to the word *vita*, meaning "to know". The word "wise" here probably refers to a type of divine wisdom attained through divination or mediumship. Thus, a *Vitka/Vitki* was a medium who attained wisdom through invocation and evocation of the Gods and *Volva* and *Vitka/Vitki* can be considered the Nordic equivalents of the Anglo-Saxon *Wicca* and *Wicce*. Price (2002) explores *Seiðr* and the roles of *Volur* in Norse society, noting their use of staffs and ritualised prophecy. Strömbäck (1975) examines Old Norse sources to trace the ritual elements of *Seiðr*, emphasising the centrality of prophecy and trance states.

In the Norse sagas, the *Volur* and *Vitkar* would perform *Seiðr* while seated. During this rite, they channelled the Gods, spirits of the dead and divine energy. This type of invocation and evocation can be an ecstatic experience, whereby the *Volva/Vitka/Vitki*/Witch becomes one with the divine, receiving visions, insights and communicating messages from the spirit realm. The chair a *Volva* sat on while performing *Seiðr* was called a *seiðhjallr* (Price 2002). Sometimes the Volva would be seated on a high platform (Price 2002). Sitting while performing mediumship parallels the modern seance, where the medium is seated while invoking or evoking spirits to deliver messages to the living.

The Old Norse literature and archaeological evidence from Nordic countries and England also indicate that practitioners of divination and magic made use of staffs and wands. The name *Volva* itself means "staff-bearer" (Price 2002:112). Staffs were made either of wood or metal (Price 2002).

WICCACRAFT

The Witch's wand and staff were used for various purposes in pre-Christian Europe. However, in modern Wiccacraft, the wand is primarily used to direct energy, for example, when casting circles.

There are numerous mentions in Old Norse texts about the *Volva's* ability for divination and foresight. They would address an entire household, community or individuals while performing *Seiðr*. There is also one story of *Volur* performing *Seiðr* only with other *Volur* present (Price 2002). The insights gained from *Seiðr* were communicated to the household the following morning (Price 2002). In *Erik's Saga*, a *Volva* has the ability to perform divination and determine an individual's fate (Price 2002). She can also predict the weather, as does a *Volva* in *Orvar-Odds Saga* (Price 2002).

The role of a *Volva* was, therefore, to both engage in divination and bring blessings to those who consulted them. They acted as a mediator between the Gods and humanity. In a similar manner to the Anglo-Saxon *Wiccan*, it is likely that when a *Volva* divined an individual's fate they would be advising on how a person could bring harmony back to their life. This type of divination was a diagnosis, where a *Volva*/Witch could see if the individual's life was in chaos or unstable. The *Volva* could then remedy the issue through prayer, ritual, magic or herbalism.

The History and Etymology of Witchcraft

Witchcraft, *Seiðr* and Homosexuality

Odin/Woden, the main God of the Germanic pantheon, was strongly associated with *Seiðr*/Witchcraft and like other *Vitkar*, he embodied gender-nonconforming traits. In the Poetic Edda, it is also said that Odin slept with men when he manifested as a *Vitka* (Bray 1908). Throughout Europe, Witchcraft has always been practised by men and women. However, in general, men who engaged in Witchcraft did not adhere to heteronormative constructs of gender and, like women, these men were considered to be receptive to spiritual forces. Gay or gender-nonconforming people have an excellent capacity for accessing the divine in that they are likely to have embraced who they are and to be acutely aware that societal norms and expected behaviour are socially constructed. Once this realisation has been made, it is possible to access the God and Goddess within oneself. They are visceral forces that are manifested by embracing feelings and sensations rather than oppressing them by adhering to a set of norms that may be dissonant with an individual's feeling of self.

The *Goetes* and *Manteis* - Ancient Greek Ecstatic Mediums Of The Gods

The Ancient Greek term for Witchcraft was *Goeteia* (Γοητεια), translated as "Goetia" in Modern English. The term *Manteia* (Μαντεια) refers to the Ancient Greek practice of divinatory Witchcraft, whereby seers, mediums and diviners, known as *Manteis* (Μαντεις), were possessed by the Gods, during which they would experience divine ecstasy/*ekstasis* (εκστασις) and deliver messages and solutions to those who consulted them. Witches, known as *Goetes* (Γοητες), were practitioners of *Manteia* who were associated with Chthonic Deities. Chthonic deities were Gods and Goddesses associated with the Underworld, death and rebirth, such as Hecate, Persephone and Dionysus. The mythical Witch Circe was a practitioner of Goetic rites and the Greek Magical Papyri which date from 100 BCE to the 5th century were written by practitioners of *Goeteia*. Luck (2006) describes *Goeteia* as a form of chthonic magic involving necromancy, binding spells and lamentation rituals to summon or appease spirits. Burkert (1985) situates Goeteia within the broader religious life of Ancient Greece, associating it with ritual specialists and beliefs about *daimones*. The Ancient Greek word *daemon/daimon* (δαίμων) (where we get the Modern English word "demon" from) was a neutral term that meant "spirit" or "divine being". It often referred to nature spirits such as nymphs and satyrs, but it was also used to refer to Gods and Goddesses. It only developed evil connotations after the Greeks converted to Christianity. Foster (2010) analyses *Manteia* as

THE HISTORY AND ETYMOLOGY OF WITCHCRAFT

prophetic practice which involved working with divine or *daimonic* forces, often tied to seers in Greek cultural life.

The singular of *Goetes* is *Goes* (Γοης). *Goeteia* and *Goes* are related to the word *goan* (γοαν) meaning to "sing a lament" (Johnston 2008:14). This reflects the association of the *Goetes* with the underworld and that they would wail or shriek while going into trance. The shrieking and wailing of the *Goetes* would open the gates of the Underworld and call on the Chthonic Deities to guide the spirits of the dead to the Underworld. *Goeteia* was strongly associated with the Goddess Hecate and her followers.

The *Goetes* operated outside of the Greek state and therefore they were seen as threatening to the Greek establishment and social control. They offered people a direct and personal connection with the divine, that was not controlled by established institutions.

In addition to divination and communicating messages to people through possession by the Gods, the *Goetes* would also perform rituals and spells for those who consulted them to bind enemies (in order for protection), to bring good luck and to restore harmony.

A *Goes* helped people maintain a relationship with the Gods to ensure that the living could sustain a harmonious life in which they lived in equilibrium with the divine. They were said to have knowledge of the Underworld and they would give people advice on how to ensure that their soul would be fully integrated with the spirit realm after death. The *Goetes* placed emphasis on fully embodying the Chthonic/Underworld Deities whilst in trance, indicating that they did not view divinity as something separate from the physical.

The God Dionysus, while disguised as one of his followers, is referred to as a "*Goes*" in the 405 BCE play The Bacchae, written by Euripides. The play makes a connection between *Goeteia* and "ecstatic mystery-rites" (Dickie 2003:33).

The Ancient Greek mystic Orpheus was initiated into the practice of *Goeteia*. According to legend, he is said to have travelled to the Underworld, where he gained sacred knowledge (Johnston 2008). He passed on this arcane knowledge through initiating other people into *Goeteia*. His teachings emphasised connection with the God Dionysus and the Goddess Persephone, both deities of death and rebirth, indicating the importance in Goeteia of a spiritual death and rebirth in order to fully access the divinity within ourselves and the universe.

The *Goetes* were an example of how one of the core aspects of Witchcraft was the invocation and evocation of the Gods and spirits of the dead, a type of Pagan mediumship that involved direct connection with the divine in the form of spiritual ecstasy and awakening our true spiritual selves.

The term *Mageia* was later introduced into the Greek language from Persian as another word for Witchcraft. *Mageia* was used interchangeably with *Goeteia* and its practitioners were known as *Magoi* (plural), *Magos* (Male) and *Magissa* (female). The term *Goeteia* was still used in the Byzantine Empire (the Greek-speaking Eastern Roman Empire) as a term for the practice of summoning spirits and it is found in a 10th century lexicon called the *Suda* (Dickie 2003).

Witches in Ancient Greece were also known by a variety of other names, including *Nekyomantis* (later called *Nekromantis*) and *Psychagogos*. The Greek terminology was adopted into Latin by the Romans.

The possession of *Goetes* by the Gods as well as the divination they performed was known as *Manteia*. *Manteia* did not have to be *Goetic* in nature; it was a generic terms for possession by the Gods and for divination. The *Goetes* were specifically practitioners of *Manteia* associated with the Chthonic Deities of the Underworld, death and rebirth, while other practitioners of *Manteia* worked with different deities. The singular of *Manteis* is *Mantis* (Μαντις). *Manteis* and *Manteia* are related to the word *mainomai* (μαινομαι), which means to "be mad" or "raving". This reflects the association of the *Manteis* with divine madness, where they would fully embody the energy of the Gods possessing them while in trance and speak in ways that were sometimes difficult for others to understand. The speech could be fast, sound like it came from the stomach or roared. While in this state of trance, it was believed that the *Manteis* could become one with the universal divine energy known to the Ancient Greeks as "the One" (Luck 2006). *Manteia* was considered a divine calling that would lead to spiritual fulfilment when answered.

Manteia was also a general term for divination (the English suffix mancy, meaning "divination", is derived from *Manteia*) and in addition to the Gods speaking through them through possession and trance, the *Mantis* would also deliver messages and predictions by throwing lots, such as sticks or bones (Luck 2006). The purpose of *Manteia* was not to predict an unchangeable fatalistic future, but instead it was used to analyse a querent's present and potential future circumstances and to discover what methods could be used to improve these circumstances. A commonly suggested method of improving a querent's situation was to make an offering to the Gods.

The *Manteis* performed ritual purification, including purifying those who were about to participate in rituals of the Orphic-Bacchic Mysteries (Dickie 2003). Dionysus is further associated with *Goeteia* and *Manteia* as the God of divine ecstasy and divine madness.

The followers of the Eleusinian Mysteries practised *Manteia* in the form of possession by the Goddesses Persephone and Demeter during their ceremonies. The Goddess Hecate and her followers are also associated with *Goeteia* and *Manteia*, as she is an Underworld deity of esoteric wisdom which can be accessed through the practise of mediumship and divination.

The *Goetes* were an example of how one of the core aspects of Witchcraft was the invocation and evocation of the Gods, a type of Pagan mediumship that involved direct connection with the divine in the form of spiritual ecstasy and awakening our true spiritual selves.

A Summary of the History and Terminology of Witchcraft in Pre-Christian Pagan Europe

From the literary sources and linguistic studies, it is evident that Witchcraft and its specialists, known as *Wiccan* in Anglo-Saxon England, *Vitkar/Volur* in Norse lands and *Goetes/Manteis* in Ancient Greece, were diviners who invoked and evoked the Gods and various spirits to obtain wisdom and insights. In Anglo-Saxon England this practice was known as *Wiccecræft*, while in Nordic lands it was known as *Seiðr* and in Ancient Greece it was called *Goeteia* and *Manteia*. These religious specialists were also found throughout other Indo-European cultures. The Irish word for this specialist was *Drui* and in Welsh this type of practitioner was called a *Dryw*. These words and practices indicate a shared Indo-European heritage of magical and divinatory practice. The overlap between *Wiccecræft*, *Seiðr*, *Goeteia* and *Manteia* reflect the interconnectedness of magical traditions across early European cultures.

The Denigration of Witchcraft

While the practices of Witchcraft were officially forbidden after Europeans converted to Christianity, Witches did continue to practise in secret and in some areas, they were openly tolerated. They were still consulted by community members in matters relating to the future and provided charms to improve luck and wellbeing. The perception of Witchcraft as a practice connected to the Devil had already been mentioned in various legal texts shortly after conversion, but viewing Witches as Devil worshippers was not widespread among the common folk. Those who did have negative attitudes towards Witches generally thought they were deluded for thinking they had access to divine power that was not mediated through a Christian

Church. However, the attitude towards Witches started to drastically change to one of hostility and they came to be seen as agents of the Devil. This process of vilification had started in the 14th century and it came at a time when Christian churches became paranoid about different interpretations of Christianity and religion that were starting to emerge. Some of the earliest examples of this include the persecution and execution of the Cathars and the Knights Templar. They, while Christian, practised a form of Christianity that was seen as heretical by the Catholic church. Protestant Christianity emerged in the 16th century and became widespread in many European countries, where it replaced Catholicism, particularly in what is now known as northern Germany, England, Wales, Scotland, Denmark, Sweden, Norway, Iceland, the Netherlands, Finland and specific areas of France, Belgium and Switzerland. The conflict between these two interpretations of Christianity led to widespread violent clashes throughout Europe. Both Protestants and Catholics became suspicious of anyone who was seen as a threat to their religious denomination. This suspicion resulted in Witches being heavily stigmatised. They were an example of people who did not believe that their connection to the divine needed to be accessed through a Christian church and its priests. Between the 14th and 18th centuries, approximately 50,000 people were executed due to accusations of practising Witchcraft (DK 2020). The majority of these people were not Witches or people who practised magic or divination in any way. They were often people disliked by the community or people who did not conform to or fit in with the norms of the communities in which they resided. The persecution occurred in both rural and urban areas. Both women and men were persecuted and they were both referred to as Witches during their trials.

Despite the widespread targeting of Witches, some did continue to practise divination and create charms. In some areas of England, they were referred to as White Witches or Cunning Folk. By the 18th century, the Witchcraft hysteria had started to die down, but the practice was still illegal. The 18th century saw the beginning of the period known as the Enlightenment, which was characterised by intellectual philosophy and reasoning through logic. The Enlightenment era resulted in people coming to view Witchcraft as not something associated with the Devil. Instead, Witches were seen as somewhat deluded individuals who erroneously thought they had access to magical power and new laws were enacted that prevented people from consulting them. It was now illegal to consult Witches because it was seen as an illogical practice that had no actual effect on the lives of the people who consulted them. In England, this law came in the form of the *Witchcraft Act of 1735*. It was only repealed in 1951.

The Emergence of Modern Witchcraft and Neopaganism

The pre-Christian Pagan practices of divination, charms, spells and mediumship continued and survived during the persecution of Witches in the post-conversion era of Europe. However, it had primarily become a fragmented and secret practice. Its practitioners were generally solitary and there is not much evidence to indicate that Witches were members of covens in the Christian era. Evidence from the pre-Christian Pagan era does indicate that some Witches worked in groups, as is seen in the examples of the *Volur* and *Vitkar* of the Nordic countries. However, this is not akin to the imaginary covens made up by Christian writers between the 14th and 17th centuries.

In addition to the survival of divination, mediumship, spells and charms, the Pagan seasonal festivals survived through folk traditions. In the 19th century, there became increasing academic interest in folklore, Paganism and Witchcraft. This resulted in the formation of covens and societies that incorporated elements of folk traditions, mythology and Medieval/Renaissance Ceremonial Magic. These developments set the foundations of a modern Witchcraft religion known as Wicca.

The Neo-Pagan religion of Wicca was founded by Gerald Gardner, an English anthropologist who had been initiated into a Pagan coven in 1939 in the New Forest in Hampshire, England. He claimed that this coven used the word *Wicca* to refer to its members. He believed that this coven was a survival of a Neolithic Pagan religion. He recorded the rituals and ceremonies of this group and incorporated elements of Ceremonial Magic into these writings. He used this framework to create Wicca, which was made public with his publication of *The Meaning of Witchcraft* in 1959, after the *Witchcraft Act of 1735* had been repealed. His student Doreen Valiente was instrumental in expanding on these works and disseminating Wicca to the broader public. One of his later students, Raymond Buckland, played a significant role in introducing the religion to America. Wicca incorporates traditions that have survived through folk practices, such as the celebration of eight Pagan seasonal festivals and the idea of one God and Goddess representing all Pagan Deities. It emphasises the life cycle of the God and Goddess, which Wiccans see as being metaphors for the change of the seasons, which are celebrated during the seasonal festivals. Wicca also incorporates divination and spell work from a variety of traditions and cultures. Wicca, therefore, has elements of pre-Christian Pagan Witchcraft, but it is not identical to it.

Wiccacraft, the type of Pagan Witchcraft presented in this book, incorporates elements of Wicca, such as celebrating the eight seasonal festivals, the ritual items and tools used for practising Witchcraft, adhering to the ethics of the *Wiccan Rede* and viewing the God and Goddess as being representative of all Deities. Wiccacraft, however, associates the eight seasonal festivals with the manifestation of the God and Goddess as specifically named deities, who can be associated with the nature of each festival. Wiccacraft also incorporates the mediumship techniques of the Pagan Witches of pre-Christian Europe by emphasising invocation and evocation of the Gods and Goddesses. Wiccacraft places importance on the Witch's personal relationship with the Gods, which is achieved through prayer and intuition. Witches are called to be Witches and Wiccacraft emphasises self-initiation directly through the God and Goddess, rather than initiation through covens. The God and Goddess are viewed as being one with us and it uses techniques to awaken the divine within ourselves. Wiccacraft uses divination techniques attested in Pagan literary sources and views divination as a means to determine a variety of future outcomes that can be changed through ritual and magic. It roots Witchcraft in Pagan agricultural/agrarian societies and returns the word

"Witch" to its original meaning of Pagan diviner and medium.

The Theology of Wiccacraft

The Differences Between Witchcraft and Shamanism

Witchcraft is not the same as Shamanism, but there are some similarities. Shamanism refers to the spiritual practices of Siberian people and all related peoples, including Native Americans. Shamanism was and is practised by hunter-gatherer societies, whereas Witchcraft and Paganism emerged from agricultural-agrarian cultures. Like Witches, Shamans are religious specialists within a wider religion. Shamanism is characterised by the Shaman leaving their body and entering the spirit world to connect with the divine and perform healing. Witchcraft and Paganism emphasise both invoking and evoking Gods and Goddesses and entering the spirit realm. Eliade (1964) emphasises that shamanic ecstasy involves the soul's journey to the spirit world, contrasting with witchcraft's focus on drawing deities into the practitioner.

Witchcraft and Paganism differ from Shamanism in that Paganism views Gods and Goddesses as personifications of natural forces, while Shamans place less emphasis on Deities. The Deities of Pagan Witches are often personified in human or anthropomorphic form. In Paganism, there is a lot of focus on fertility Deities, as Pagan societies were agricultural and depended on the successful growth and harvesting of crops. In contrast, Shamanic cultures were focused on hunting and gathering. As discussed in the previous chapter, Witches were diviners and mediums of Deities. The purpose of the Pagan Witch was to diagnose through divination and perform healing through spell work and charms. They aimed to bring calmness back to people's lives. Witches also delivered messages from the Deities, in the form of mediumship, to the community. They also played a role in celebrating the eight European seasonal festivals, during which they would invoke the Gods.

The God and Goddess

In Wiccacraft/Witchcraft, the God and Goddess are the two aspects of a universal energy present in everything. This universal unifying spiritual force is sometimes referred to as the One. In Ancient Greece, certain Greek Pagans, namely the Neo-Platonists, believed that this universal force could not be named and therefore they referred to it as the One. All Gods and Goddesses were seen as being an aspect of this divine energy. Belief in the One as the source of all Deities was present throughout Pagan Indo-European cultures.

The God and Goddess together constitute the whole of the One. The God and Goddess are not separate beings but are two parts of the same being. The God is in the Goddess and the Goddess is in the God. They can be thought of as two sides of the same coin. All Gods are aspects of the God and all Goddesses are aspects of the Goddess. By connecting with the God and Goddess in Witchcraft, we connect with the universal divine energy that constitutes everything in the natural world.

Early Anglo-Saxon religious beliefs, as reconstructed from both archaeological items and literature, viewed the world as being inhabited by a variety of divine beings. These included not only the deities of the Germanic people (such as Woden/Odin), but also land-spirits such as Elves (*Ælfe*) and protective household entities, which appear in charms and blessing rituals (Jolly 1996).

In Norse religion, there was a belief in Nine Worlds ruled by the Aesir and Vanir Deities and there was a belief that practitioners of *Seiðr* acted as mediators between humans and the divine (Price 2004). The God Woden/Odin sacrificed himself for wisdom, which is also symbolises the spiritual death and rebirth of the Witch in order to gain divine knowledge. In Ancient Greece, there was also a variety of divine beings, including Olympian Deities, Chthonic (Underworld) Deities and *Daimones*, the latter being nature spirits such as Satyrs and Nymphs. Practitioners of *manteia* were vessels of divine will. The overlap between these belief systems and practices reflects Witchcraft's Indo-European theological roots.

In Witchcraft, nature and the universe are one with the divine. Witchcraft can therefore be described as pantheistic. In Ancient Greece, a belief in universal divine energy was referred to as Monism. This belief is not the same as monotheism. Monotheism is the belief in one God, but this God is seen as a separate and distinct entity from nature and the universe.

On the other hand, in Monism, nature and the universe are one with the divine. As discussed above, the God and Goddess constitute the totality of the divine and all other Deities are, in turn, aspects of them. The saying in Hermeticism (which is related to Monism), "As above, so below", refers to the fact that everything in the universe is connected. The earth is one with the heavens. The divine realm is not separate from the earth. Through connecting with the earth, we connect with the Gods. In the same vein, the divine is also present in the heavens. Through connecting with celestial objects such as the moon and the sun, we also connect with the Gods. Witchcraft is about connecting with the Deities through nature and realising the divinity of the universe. Those who have been called to be Witches can find fulfilment through connecting with the forces of nature, as the Gods are personifications of the forces of nature.

Linguistically, the names of Gods are often connected to the words of the forces that they personify. For example, the names of the sky Gods Zeus (Greek), Jupiter (Roman) and Tiwaz (Norse) are descended from the Proto-Indo-European word *Dyeus*, meaning "Sky". Therefore, our Pagan ancestors viewed the Gods and Goddesses as the personification of the natural world. Through performing a spell or ritual connected with a specific Deity, we can effect changes in our lives and connect with a particular aspect of the divine that the God or Goddess you are working with represents.

In Witchcraft, the God is often depicted as a horned God, as in pre-Christian Pagan Europe, the Gods most associated with Witchcraft were horned Gods, such as Woden/Odin and Dionysus. Like the God, the Goddess has many aspects. In Wiccacraft, she is called upon as Hecate, Artemis, Selene, Persephone, Diana, Demeter, Freya and Frigg. Witches honour and embody the God and Goddess as the Deities of the moon, sun, spirit realm, Underworld, night and fertility of the earth. They are called upon for divine knowledge and wisdom, to experience religious ecstasy through becoming one with them, to awaken the divine within ourselves and to become our true self. The eight seasonal festivals celebrated in Wiccacraft are associated with specific Deities. Both the God and Goddess have triple aspects. In Ancient Greece, the Gods Zeus, Poseidon and Hades were sometimes seen as being three parts of the same Deity (Uzdavinys 2004), while the Goddesses Hecate, Artemis and Selene were often seen as a Triple Goddess.

In pre-Christian Pagan Europe, it was the norm for Pagans to equate the Gods of their own cultures with the Gods of other Pagan cultures. The Romans equated Diana with the Greek Goddesses Hecate, Artemis and Selene. The Greek Dionysus was equated with the Roman God Liber and was also worshipped as Bacchus (from Greek Bakkhos). Zeus was equated with Jupiter. The Greek Goddess Persephone was equated with Libera, who was later called Prosperina. As a result of the Roman empire expanding into Germanic and Celtic Europe, the various cultures that interacted with each other saw their Gods as the same beings but known by different names. This equivalence resulted in the building of temples where both the Roman and local names of Deities were used when referring to the same entity. Most of these Deities have the same Indo-European origin. Like modern Wiccans, they recognised a universal divinity that was worshipped by many different names.

The Theology of Wiccacraft

In Wiccacraft, the Deities are addressed as "God and Goddess", "Lord and Lady" and "the Old Gods" or specific Deity names will be used, such as Woden or Hecate or a combination of both, depending on the ritual.

You can find a more detailed account of the specific Gods and Goddesses of Wiccacraft and the hymns you can use to invoke, evoke or connect with them in the chapter on Gods and Goddesses.

The Calling to be a Witch - Self-Initiation or Coven Initiation

Witches have a divine calling by the Gods to practise Witchcraft. Witches are born Witches. In numerous cultures worldwide, those who become mediums/diviners have a calling to this path and the same principle applies to Witches. When this calling is answered, by undergoing initiation, a Witch will feel spiritually fulfilled, connected to the God and Goddess and strong and more stable within their lives. Initiation does not resolve or fix everything wrong in your life, but it will make you feel like you are fully walking on your true path, which will lead to divine connection, awakening the divine from within and insight into your life.

Anyone drawn to Pagan Witchcraft who feels like it is the right path for them has a calling to become a Witch. Witches can self-initiate. In mediumship and divination traditions in Africa, some mediums/diviners are taught directly through the Gods and ancestors through intuition and dreams on how to self-initiate, which herbs to use in ritual, which songs to sing while in a trance and how to practise divination. Mediums/diviners who are taught in this way usually start their own lodges. It is from these people that all lodges in specific African traditions are descended.

The same is true for Witchcraft. There are Witches who are solitary practitioners who self-initiate and who learn from the Gods through intuition, prayer, invocation and evocation. Self-initiation is the approach that Wiccacraft, encourages. Other Witches are initiated into and learn through "covens".

The word "coven" was used by anthropologist Margaret Murray in her work *The Witch-Cult in Western Europe* (1921) to describe a gathering of Witches. I use the term "lodge" as well as "coven" when referring to Witches belonging to the same group and lineage. In the pre-Christian era, there were always Witches who were solitary and Witches who were part of lodges. Those in lodges would assist each other in activities such as drumming to induce trance, administering certain herbs to other members for magical purposes and teaching divination and ceremonies to their students. Again, it must be stated that all lodges would have had individual founders who were solitary Witches.

After the conversion to Christianity in European countries, almost all Witches became solitary practitioners. Being part of a lodge in a land where Witchcraft was outlawed would have been very risky due to the attention it would draw. Witchcraft was therefore kept alive by solitary practitioners in times when it was persecuted. However, the memory of Witchcraft lodges survived, which is why they were frequently featured in the accusations made by Church officials against people who were thought to be involved in Witchcraft.

Lodges started to form again in the 19th century, when Folklore Studies, Religious Studies, Anthropology and Archaeology began to take off as academic fields. Those who felt an affinity for Witchcraft and Paganism would have read these materials and incorporated this knowledge with their knowledge of surviving folk rituals, ceremonies and magic into their practices. This resulted in the formation of new lodges/covens, which would ultimately lead to the birth of modern Wicca and other Neopagan Witchcraft traditions.

Divination and Magic

As discussed earlier, Witches were religious specialists (diviners and mediums) within a Pagan religious system. Witches would have had a central role in helping people stay connected to the Gods by interpreting their messages through divination, intuition and invocation/evocation. Once the Witch had assessed a situation through these means, they would perform the appropriate solution. The resolution could be in the form of a prayer or offering to the Gods or the use of charms, magical herbs and spells. They would summon the Gods in all of these circumstances to assist them and channel their divine energy. Sometimes a Deity would speak through a Witch if they were invoked. These actions would bring harmony back into a person's life, as harmony was seen as the natural order of things. Pagans did not view bad luck, poverty, continuous suffering and hardship as being the will of the Gods. It was the role of the Witches to help people afflicted with these conditions. Using magic would have given an individual a sense of hope and strength. It would assist them in achieving their desired outcome by awakening these traits within themselves while simultaneously harnessing the energy associated with the charms, herbs and Gods that were called on. The Witch also performed magic for themselves. The Witch did this to ensure that they maintained wholeness in their life and their connection to the Gods.

In Wiccacraft, magic is performed by Witches for themselves. However, it is up to the individual if they wish to assist others by using magic. Wiccacraft is about maintaining a connection with the God and Goddess for spiritual fulfilment, sustaining a link to the divinity of nature and answering the calling to become a Witch by becoming one with the God and Goddess. If you do perform magic for others, you should ideally do it for free. The assistance to someone seeking your help will be reciprocated in the form of feeling fulfilled within yourself. If you want some form of payment, it would be better to request something that could be offered to the Gods, such as cider, beer, wine or juice, which you can consume after presenting some as an offering to the Deities. These offerings are a better option than accepting money. If you insist on charging money, offer the money to the God and Goddess before using it. Once you have presented it and stated that it is payment for the services you have provided as a Witch, leave it on the altar until the next day when you can use it. Remember, all the work you are doing as a Witch is through the God and Goddess, who are one with you. They are in you; you are in them. Therefore, any type of payment for the work you do as a Witch should first be presented as an offering.

Offerings and Divine Reciprocity

In pre-Christian times, offerings were given as a way of maintaining relationships with the Gods. A reciprocal bond is created between the Gods and humanity through providing an offering. The Gods were believed to bless humanity through the growth of crops and a successful harvest. The life force leading to this fertility and growth can be seen as divine productive energy from the Gods that circulates through the community. It spreads through exchange and trade between community members in the form of the harvested goods and various created items. Through offerings, this productive energy is given back to the Gods and so the cycle begins again. Thus, through this exchange, we develop connections with the divine, land, animals and others. The Gods can be seen as metaphors for the natural forces that make this kind of production and labour possible. Through offerings, Witches give thanks to the divine, in other words, nature, for all that it provides them. Offerings can include cider, beer, mead, fruit, grains etc. Animal sacrifice is not a part of modern Witchcraft or the Wiccacraft form of Witchcraft I have presented in this book. Reciprocal relations with the Gods are possible through the offering of goods derived solely from vegetation.

Furthermore, Wiccacraft incorporates the Wiccan Rede written by Gardnerian Wiccans, stating, "An it harm none, do what ye will." What is most important is that you are honouring and giving thanks for all that nature has provided for you and the reciprocal relationship between you, the Gods and nature.

The Spirit Realm

In pre-Christian Pagan Europe, the spirit realm was not seen as a transcendent place inaccessible to the living. The world of the dead was very much tied to the earth and the living. Most European Pagan cultures viewed the spirits of the deceased as entering the Underworld after death. When we die and are buried, our body decomposes and becomes one with the earth. We become part of the soil, the trees, rivers, oceans, mounds, hills, mountains and the air. Our essence returns to the divine, which is nature itself. This process was personified as the Underworld due to our bodies becoming part of the earth when we die. In many European cultures, the dead and the spirit realm were associated with mounds, hills, forests, rivers and the ocean. Through connecting with nature, we connect with the spirits of the deceased and the Gods, who are one.

Symbols of Wiccacraft

The Pentagram

The upward-pointing pentagram is the main symbol of Wiccacraft/Witchcraft. The pentagram represents the five elements of earth, air, fire, water and aether, which Ancient Greek philosophers such as Plato and Aristotle believed constituted the totality of the universe. The followers of Pythagoras used it as a symbol of health and wellbeing. The pentagram has also been found at ancient sites throughout Europe and was most often found near graves and in caves. This indicates that it was possibly linked to the spirit realm.

The Triple Moon

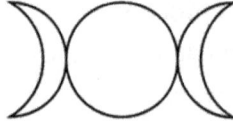

The triple moon is the symbol of the Greek Triple Goddess Hecate-Artemis-Selene. It is also the symbol of the Roman Goddess Diana, an amalgamation of these three Greek Goddesses. As a Triple Goddess, these Goddesses symbolise Witchcraft, the Underworld and spirits of the dead, the moon, forests and untamed wilderness.

The Triskelion

Like the pentagram, the triskelion has been used throughout Europe since ancient times. In

Wiccacraft, it is the symbol of the Triple God. In the Anglo-Saxon and Norse pantheon, this is Woden/Odin-Thunar/Thor-Frey/Ing, representing the spirit realm, earth and sky. In the Greek pantheon, the Triple God is Zeus-Poseidon-Hades, representing the realms of the sky, ocean and Underworld.

Ritual Items and Tools

The Historical use of tools in pagan witchcraft

Archaeological and literary evidence indicate that ritual tools have been used for religious and symbolic purposes by various Indo-European cultures. In Anglo-Saxon culture, iron knives, staffs and chalices have been found in both graves and ritual sites, which indicates they may have been used in religious contexts (Hamerow et al. 2011). Staffs have been found in numerous burials of high status Anglo-Saxon women, which parallels the staffs used by the Norse *Volva*, which was a symbol of magical ability (Price 2004). The Norse Sagas indicate that practitioners of *Seiðr* used ritual platforms, staffs and bespoke cloaks to facilitate going into trance to deliver messages from the divine (Mitchell 2011). These tools created sacred spaces and directed magical power. In Ancient Greek ritual, items such as offering bowls, tree branches and incense burners were used in *Manteia* and *Goeteia* practices (Luck 2006). These examples from various Indo-European cultures reflect the widespread historical use of sacred objects to direct magical intent and to invoke and evoke divine beings in Witchcraft.

Altar

The altar is the place where most Wiccacraftian rituals and ceremonies take place. You can create an altar on a table, a chest of drawers, a bedside table or a chest, among other things. The altar should be at a height that enables you to sit cross-legged, facing it while engaged in your ritual activities. As has been discussed in previous chapters dealing with the practice of *Wiccecræft*, *Seiðr* and *Goeteia* among Pagan Witches in pre-Christian Europe, rites that involved invoking and evoking the Gods began while seated.

Ideally, it would help if you had an altar that can also store your ritual items, such as a chest of drawers or a cabinet. You should also be able to cast a circle around the altar so that you can use it while in the sacred circle. This means that you might have to move your altar to a more central position in the room if the altar usually stands against the wall. If this is not possible, you can gather the specific items you need for a ritual from your altar and use them in the area where you will perform the rite, after which you can return them to the altar. You can also do this if you have a garden and want to conduct your rites outdoors.

Certain ritual items and symbols should remain atop the altar, while others can be packed away until they are needed in a ritual. Deity candles, symbols or representations of the God and

Goddess, an incense holder, a bowl of water, a bowl of salt, an offering bowl, your wand and the chalice should continually be kept on top of the altar. If it is not possible to do this, then you can keep your sacred items stored in a chest of drawers or a cupboard, where they will not be disturbed. If this is what you need to do, say a prayer to the God and Goddess, explaining to them that it is not possible due to your circumstances to keep your ritual items atop your altar. Explain to them where you will keep their symbols instead.

The altar should have a cloth covering it, which will need to be washed from time to time. This can be made of cotton, velvet, satin or any fabric that you feel is appropriate. The cloth should be in a colour that resonates with you and one that you feel will be conducive to your Wiccacraftian practice.

Deity Candles

The Deity candles are used for calling on the God and Goddess. They are the physical and spiritual representation of the Deities and lighting them indicates that you are asking them to be present and both to participate in and listen to your rites and prayers.

The Goddess candle should be in the back left corner of the altar. The candle should be in a colour that represents the Goddess for you. I use a silver candle, as silver symbolises the moonlight of the Goddess.

The right side of the altar is the side of the God and a candle representing him should be placed in the back right corner. I use a black candle to represent the God, to signify his manifestation as Lord of the night, the secrets of the runes and the spirit realm. Between these two candles, in the centre, should be a white candle representing the One. Together the God and Goddess form a universal whole representing everything in the natural world and this white candle signifies that union. I use taper candles in candle holders for the God and Goddess, as some rituals involve moving these candles. The centre candle usually stays in its position and therefore it does not need to be easily mobile.

Symbols of the God and Goddess

The altar should have symbols on it that represent the God and Goddess, in addition to the Deity candles. For the Goddess, these can be seashells, selenite crystals, statues representing her or a specific Goddess, lunar symbols, such as a triple moon pendant or decoration, ornaments or decorative items of apples, pomegranates; anything you feel represents her for you. Some of the things you can use as symbols of the God include artificial antlers, jet crystals, statues or pendants of horned Gods, the Ansuz ᚠ rune (which is a symbol of the God Woden/Odin the All-Father) and ornaments of grapes, vine leaves or pinecones, representing Dionysus. Remember to choose symbols that represent the God and Goddess for you.

Wand

The wand is used for directing energy during Wiccacraftian rituals and ceremonies. The power of the God and Goddess flows through us into the wand, through which it can be directed. The wand is used for casting circles and focusing magical energy on a specific point. Wands should be made either of wood or metal. I use a wand made from the wood of the ash tree, as the ash tree represents the World Tree known as Yggdrasil in Norse mythology. In the *Havamal* section of the *Poetic Edda*, the God Odin/Woden hangs from Yggdrasil to undergo a spiritual death and rebirth to gain divine wisdom. Archaeological and literary evidence indicates that wands were valuable tools used by Witches in Germanic Northern European countries, such as England, Iceland, Norway, Sweden and Denmark. The Witch should keep the wand on the altar, near the front and in the centre. You can make your wand by collecting branches or twigs or you can buy one already made. Once you have blessed your wand or any other ritual item, it becomes yours; therefore, buying premade tools is not an issue. Your wand does not need to be decorated or engraved, but you can carve your wand with runes and other symbols meaningful to you if you want to.

Incense and Incense Holder

Incense is used to call on the Gods and is used in most Wiccacraftian rituals and ceremonies, whether during a seasonal festival such as Yule or a daily prayer to the God and Goddess. Incense calls on the Deities and seals in/reinforces their divine energy when casting circles, blessing tools and performing cleansings. It brings the divine power of the Old Gods into a space. The incense that has been used in Pagan rituals for centuries includes sandalwood, frankincense, myrrh and European/common sage. You can use incense sticks, cones or resin. If you are using sage or another herb, you can burn it on the top of a charcoal disc. You will also need an incense holder, also known as a censer, to burn the incense. If you use stick incense, you can find wooden incense holders that hold multiple burning incense sticks at once, which is very effective for rituals.

Water Bowl

A Witch should always keep a bowl of water on their altar. When mixed with salt, it is used to cleanse and bless spaces and people. Water is strongly associated with the spirit world. In Greek mythology, the dead had to cross the river Styx to reach the Underworld. It, therefore, represents a spiritual life force, as the dead symbolise the essence of the soul and spiritual vitality. Water is necessary for growth and life. In Wiccacraft, the Witch can use it in spells that focus on personal development or the manifestation of a goal through gradual advancement and work.

Salt Bowl

Salt has long been associated with cleansing properties. In Wiccacraft, it signifies vitality and the minerals of the earth necessary for life. A bowl of salt should be kept on your altar at all times, so it can be mixed with water to form salt water, which is used for cleansing and blessing. You can use sea salt, table salt or any salt you think will suit you in your Wiccacraftian practice.

Offering Bowl

The offering bowl is where Witches place offerings to the God and Goddess during rituals and ceremonies, such as during one of the eight seasonal festivals, a moon ritual, an invocation or evocation or whenever the Witch feels it necessary to make an offering to the Old Gods. The process of offering drink and food to the Deities is discussed in the section on the Offering Ceremony. You can draw or carve the rune Gebo X on the back of your offering bowl. This rune means gift and among the Northern European Pagans, it represented offering and reciprocity to and from the Gods. Offerings are how a Witch gives thanks to the Old Gods for providing for us. We return the energy of life to them through our offering, who in turn return it to us in the form of further growth of the earth's vegetation and crops, thus binding us together in a reciprocal relationship.

Chalice

During the Offering Ceremony to the Gods, Witches pour beverages into the chalice, recite the appropriate words for the ritual and state its intent. Some of the liquid is mixed into the offering bowl when making the offering. The Witch simultaneously keeps some in the chalice for themselves to drink. When the Witch partakes of a drink from the chalice, they take part in the joys of the ceremony with the God and Goddess and therefore the chalice is essential to Wiccacraftian ritual. It can be made of silver, gold, copper, glass or any material that appeals to you.

Silk Cord

Cord is used to create the physical outline of the sacred circle. The cord should be long enough so that it can comfortably surround you and the altar, allowing you enough space to move within it. It is better to buy a longer length of cord so that you are guaranteed to be able to cast a large circle. If the cord is too long, you can create multiple layers on top of the first circle. When you buy a roll of silk cord, you are likely to receive a cord with an extremely long length. You can deal with this by first determining the length of cord that you will need to create this circle. Once this is done, you can cut the cord and keep it in your altar for all future rituals of casting the circle. If you cannot find silk cord, then try and find another strong material. Choose a colour that you think will be conducive to your Wiccacraftian practice.

Tealight Candles

Witches use four candles to cast the circle and call on the elements. I find that tealight candles work best for this.

Anointing Oil

Anointing oil is used in initiations and ritual magic to trace the runes or other symbols on the body. It is also used in house cleansings and it acts as a form of protection and seal for the energy of the God and Goddess. When a Witch uses anointing oil for self-initiation, they are blessing themselves with the power of the God and Goddess, the Lord and Lady and the Old Gods. They affirm themselves as a Witch who has answered their calling and who is sealing the Deities' energy within themselves. To create your anointing oil, you will need olive oil, frankincense essential oil and myrrh essential oil. Frankincense was used to summon the Gods in Ancient Greece and Rome, while myrrh was used to specifically connect with the Gods of the spiritual realm and Witchcraft, such as Hecate, Dionysus and Persephone. If you cannot find these oils, try and obtain other essential oils associated with sacred blessings. You will also need a vial or a small bottle to store the mixture. Place the ingredients in front of you and say:

"God and Goddess, Lord and Lady, the Old Gods. I call to you to bless these oils of frankincense, myrrh and olive with your divinity, so they may be used to anoint, protect and strengthen all those they come into contact with. So mote it be."

Fill the vial or bottle with three-quarters of olive oil. Add twelve drops of frankincense oil and twelve drops of myrrh oil. Close the lid of the bottle or push down the cork to seal it. Shake the mixture well, visualising it as white light flowing and intertwining. When you are finished, set the oil on the altar and announce:

"God and Goddess, Lord and Lady, the Old Gods. This anointing oil has been created. May your divinity forever live within it. So mote it be."

The anointing oil should be kept in the drawers, cabinet or chest of your altar. If this is not possible, keep it somewhere safe with the other ritual items that you cannot keep in your altar.

Cauldron

The cauldron is used for mixing herbs to create potions for magical purposes. It represents the void and primordial waters from which everything came. Therefore, it is a magical generative tool where you can grow and manifest your spells through herbs. Miniature black iron cauldrons are a good option to use.

Runes

The runes are an important tool for divination and magical practice in Wiccacraft. The runes usually used are the Elder Futhark runes, which are the earliest recorded Germanic runes. The earliest examples of the Elder Futhark date back to the 2nd century. The runes will be discussed in more detail in the chapter on runes. You can buy your runes already engraved or painted or you can engrave them or paint them yourself onto stones or wood. You should keep your runes in a pouch, which you can empty onto the ground while performing divination.

Crystals

The crystals used in Wiccacraft are amethyst, quartz, selenite and jet. You can use amethyst to open yourself spiritually. Quartz represents divine knowledge and the spirit realm. Amethyst and quartz can be used in the form of a crystal ball for scrying, which is discussed in the chapter on evoking the Gods. Selenite represents the Goddess and jet represents the God and they can be used to connect with them.

Book of Rituals, Ceremonies and Divination

You can keep a book to record your adaptation of Wiccacraftian rituals and ceremonies, as well as to keep a record of spells and charms you have used. In Gardnerian Wicca, this is called a Book of Shadows. You can use this book to write down your observations during divinations and record insights and things you experience during invocation and evocation.

Ritual Clothing

During Wiccacraftian rites, it is important to wear attire that signifies that the Witch is engaged in sacred work. This can be a piece of fabric tied around the Witch's hips or waist that is ankle length or falls to the floor, similar to a sarong. I use a piece of fabric made from black velvet, as black is the colour of both the Northern European God Woden/Odin and the Greek Goddess Hecate, both Deities of Witchcraft, the spiritual realm and divine knowledge. You should choose a colour that resonates with you the most. If you feel a connection to the God Dionysus, you could select a purple fabric. If you feel close to the Goddess Demeter, then gold might be the right colour for you. You can wear this type of sarong over and with daily clothing, such as trousers, jeans, t-shirts, formal shirts, jumpers, sweatshirts, jerseys and so on. When you tie your sarong around your hips or waist, you are sending a clear message to yourself and the Gods and that you are engaged in sacred work. You can, of course, wear more elaborate clothing such as hooded cloaks if you want to.

Symbolic Jewellery

Wiccacraftian jewellery can be worn in day-to-day life, during rituals or not at all. Wearing jewellery is not an essential part of being a Witch, but for some Witches, it can make them feel closer to the God and Goddess. Witches can also use jewellery to decorate the altar. It can symbolise your connection to the God and Goddess and your identity as a Witch. You can wear it for magical reasons, such as charms for protection, good luck and strength. Jewellery can include pendants and rings of the pentagram, the triple moon and runes. Beads can be worn as bracelets around the wrists to signify connection to a specific Deity or element. Black beads could represent Woden/Odin or Hecate, purple Dionysus and white Selene. For the elements, green represents earth, white represents air, blue represents water and red represents fire. You can wear a bracelet with beads of alternating colour to represent various deities or elements or you could wear multiple bracelets with differently coloured beads for the same reason.

Cleansing Bath Ritual

You can take a cleansing bath before you perform your Wiccacraftian rituals and ceremonies. Part of Wiccacraftian practice involves making a space sacred, which entails creating a new, fresh environment to begin your ritual. Similarly, you can use a cleansing bath to cleanse yourself of the thoughts, stresses and worries you may have experienced throughout the day. The cleansing will result in you feeling refreshed and it can help you be fully present when you perform your Wiccacraftian rites. It is not essential to perform a cleansing bath before Wiccacraftian rituals, but you can if you feel that it will help you in preparing for your rituals and ceremonies.

You can use essential oils such as frankincense or myrrh or herbs such as betony, mint, fennel and thyme for your bath. Holding the oils or herbs, close your eyes and say:

> *"I ask the Old Gods to cleanse and purify me. May these oils/herbs bless me and wash away feelings of stress and worry, so that I may be relaxed and refreshed for my Wiccacraftian rites. So mote it be."*

Once you have run your bath, empty twelve drops of the essential oil into the bath or three pinches of the herbs you are using (if you have a shower instead of a bath, you can apply the oils and herbs directly to your body while showering). Feel the stress dissolve from your body as you are surrounded by the warming, purifying divinity of the herbs. You may wish to visualise the water as white light. Let any thought that comes into your mind gently disappear, so that your mind is calm and relaxed. Do not use any soap, shampoo or conditioner during this ritual. When you feel relaxed, you can drain the bath and dry yourself. You are now ready to perform your Wiccacraftian rites.

Blessing Your Tools

Your tools should be cleansed and blessed before you use them in your Wiccacraftian rituals and your initiations. You should not cast the circle or self-initiate at this stage as you still need to bless the tools required for these rites. Before blessing your tools, you should take a cleansing bath.

Your altar should be set up by now. Light the candles and incense and say:

"God and Goddess, Lord and Lady, the Old Gods. I call on you to cleanse and bless these tools so they may be used in Wiccacraftian practice. Bind me to these tools so they are mine to use. So mote it be."

Take some salt in your hands and mix it with the water in the water bowl and say:

"May the life force of the salt join with the life force of the water and bless my sacred ritual tools. So mote it be."

Take up your first object, such as the wand. Use salt water in your hands to rub onto the wand. Visualise the water covering the wand in white light as you do this. Once you have covered the object in salt water, visualise a white light flowing through your body and out of your hands into the wand. Feel the wand become a part of you. Return the water bowl to the altar. Pick up the censer with burning incense, move the fragrance around each item so that it is completely covered in smoke. As you do this, visualise the smoke sealing and reinforcing the divine energy that flowed through you, which should be visualised as white light. Once you feel ready, move onto the next ritual item and repeat the same process. This ritual needs to be done for all ritual objects, including the altar, the sarong and altar cloth. When you are finished, raise your wand pointing upwards and say:

"God and Goddess, I thank you for bearing witness to these rites. These sacred tools are now blessed, consecrated and connected to me. So mote it be."

Praying to the God and Goddess

A Witch can pray to the God and Goddess at any time. Prayers can give thanks and ask for blessings and strength, among other things. You can pray in your mind or by using spoken words. You can do this anytime and anywhere.

The following prayer is a simple ritual that you can perform at the altar. You can adapt the words of this prayer to suit your needs at the time of your prayer. If you want, you can hold selenite, representing the Goddess and jet, representing the God, in your hands while saying this prayer. Tie your ritual sarong around your waist and sit facing the altar. Light the three Deity candles and the incense. Say:

"God and Goddess, Lord and Lady, the Old Gods. I give thanks to you for all you provide for me. I pray that you surround me with your love and your light. I ask for strength and protection. I ask you to bless me, to always be with me and to bring me happiness and fulfilment. So mote it be."

When you have finished your prayer, you can remove your ritual sarong and go about your daily life. The God and Goddess have heard your prayer and are with you.

The Sacred Circle

The circle should be cast in most major Wiccacraftian rituals and ceremonies, such as celebrating the eight seasonal festivals, invocation, evocation and moon rituals. Casting the circle makes a space sacred. It creates an area separate from places used for day-to-day, profane activities. It creates a holy, divine sanctuary, where the Witch can perform their rites. It also focuses and concentrates the energy being channelled in a specific space.

Casting The Circle

Take your silk cord and create a circle with it around the altar. The altar should ideally be in the centre of the circle. Place tealight candles in the eastern, southern, western and northern parts of the circle. Return to the altar and light the three Deity candles and incense. Take up and raise your wand, pointing upwards and face the altar. Say:

"God and Goddess, Lord and Lady, the Old Gods. I call to you to bear witness to these rites and the casting of this sacred circle. So mote it be."

Place the wand on the altar. Take some salt in your hands and mix it with the water in the water bowl and say:

WICCACRAFT

> *"May the life force of the salt join with the life force of the water, so they may cleanse and bless everything they come into contact with."*

Take up your wand and point it downwards towards the east. Visualise a white light flow from your head down into your arms and through the wand. Trace a circle clockwise from the east, visualising the white light from your wand creating the circle as you move around and finish where you started. Place the wand on the altar. Take up the water bowl. Beginning in the east, sprinkle salt water all around the circle, visualising it as white light strengthening the circle. Once you have walked around the circle, sprinkling it with salt water, return the water bowl to the altar. Take up the censer with the burning incense. Starting in the east, walk around the circle with the censer, ensuring that the smoke is moved across the entirety of the circle. Visualise this also reinforcing and strengthening the light of the circle. Once completed, place the censer back on the altar. Take up the wand and lighter/matches. Light candle in the east. Stand facing east with your wand raised, stating:

> *"I call to the guardians of the watchtower of the east, spirits of air. I ask you to bear witness to these rites."*

THE SACRED CIRCLE

Use your wand to trace a pentagram in the air. Visualise this as white light moving through the end of your wand, creating a pentagram made of light.

Move to the south. Light the candle and say:

"I call to the guardians of the watchtower of the south, spirits of fire. I ask you to bear witness to these rites."

Trace a pentagram in the air with your wand, as described before.

Move to the west. Light the candle and say:

"I call to the guardians of the watchtower of the west, spirits of water. I ask you to bear witness to these rites."

Trace a pentagram in the air.

Move to the north. Light the candle and say:

"I call to the guardians of the watchtower of the north, spirits of earth. I ask you to bear witness to these rites."

Trace a pentagram in the air.

Return to the altar. Raise your wand, stating:

"God and Goddess, Lord and Lady, the Old Gods. This sacred space has now been created."

Return your wand and lighter/matches to the altar. You can now perform rituals and ceremonies within this sacred circle. Rites that should be completed within a circle should be initiations, seasonal festivals, moon rituals, invocations and evocations. You can perform magic, divination and any other Wiccacraftian practice within the sacred circle. If you need to leave the circle temporarily, you can create a doorway to exit and re-enter using your wand. To do this, hold your wand with it pointing downwards towards the ground. Lift it and trace the outline of a door. You can leave the circle using this doorway. Visualise the door as having an outline of white light. When you return to the circle, trace a pentagram in the air in the direction of the door you created. This will seal it again.

Closing the circle

Once you have finished performing your rites, it is time to close the circle. Take up your wand and stand facing the east. Raise your wand and say:

> *"God and Goddess, Lord and Lady, the Old Gods. These rites have now come to an end."*

Take your wand and thrust it into the eastern part of the circle. The circle has now been broken. The energies that were used during these rites do not need to be "cleared". They need to work through their course. Blow out the candles of the four elements, then blow out the Deity candles on the altar. You can now pack up any ritual items that need to be stored away.

The First Initiation

The First Initiation is the rite in which you will dedicate yourself to the path of Wiccacraft and the God and Goddess. It is a sacred ritual, where you answer your true calling as a Witch and which binds you to the Old Gods, becoming one with them. You do not need to be initiated by other Witches. If you have a calling to be a Witch, the God and Goddess will guide you through your intuition. If this is your calling, you already have a connection to them and they will show you the way in terms of Wiccacraftian practice and knowledge. All Witches are born Witches and have the spirit of a Witch.

It is a calling and anyone who realises that they have this calling has the right to initiate themselves through the God and Goddess. This initiation should only be undertaken if you are sure that Witchcraft is your true calling. Through this ritual, you will embody the God and Goddess and your life path will be that of a Witch, a person connected to the divine forces of nature and the divine within.

For the First Initiation, you will need to make an offering to the God and Goddess. The offering should be in the form of a drink. I use cider, but you can use beer, mead, wine or fruit juice. Choose whichever beverage you feel is suitable for this ceremony. Remember, the Gods live within you and your natural preference/tastes are a good choice for what you choose to offer.

The initiation should be performed when it feels right for you. It can be during the full moon, which symbolises fulfilment and completion or it can be performed during the new moon, symbolising new beginnings.

Before starting the initiation, you should take a cleansing bath, symbolising letting go of the past so that you are prepared for new beginnings. When you have finished the cleansing, you can begin the initiation.

You will need your anointing oil. Wear only your ritual garments during this rite, such as a plain black velvet sarong tied around your waist. This is necessary to apply the anointing oil to your body and it also signifies that you are engaged in your sacred Wiccacraftian practice.

Cast the circle in the usual manner, with the centre and Deity candles lit, as well as the incense. Remember to join the salt and water to create salt water.

Take the anointing oil, applying a good amount to your fingers. Visualise the oil as a white light.

In the centre of your forehead, draw an equilateral cross in a circle, continuing to visualise the oil as a

The First Initiation

white light. Rub the oil onto your shoulders and the back of your neck. Take more oil and draw an upward-pointing pentagram in the centre of your chest. Rub the oil on your elbows and around your wrists, on your pubic area, the top of your thighs and your ankles. Feel the oil of white light become a part of you.

Raising your wand, say:

"God and Goddess, Lord and Lady, the Old Gods. I {insert your full name} come before you to dedicate myself to you and the path of Wiccacraft. I am hereby initiated by you as a Witch, my true calling. My soul is that of a Witch and I will forever walk the path of Wiccacraft, the path of the Old Gods. I will always be one with you. I am in you, you are in me, we are one. I ask you to guide me, to always be with me, to bring me happiness, fulfilment, to keep connected with the divine in nature and within myself, for we are all one. I will always see you in the earth, the trees, the rivers, the seas, the air, the sun, the moon, the day, the night. I will abide by the Wiccan Rede of "If it harms none, do what you will." God and Goddess, Lord and Lady, the Old Gods. We are now one. For all eternity I will be dedicated to you. I am in you, you are in me. We are one. So mote it be."

Pour some of the drink into the altar chalice. Raise the chalice in your hand and say:

> *"God and Goddess, Lord and Lady, the Old Gods. I {insert your full name} have hereby been initiated into the path of a Witch, a practitioner of Wiccacraft. We are one. So mote it be."*

Pour some of the drink into the offering bowl while saying:

> *"To the Gods."*

Drink the remainder of the drink in the chalice. Take some time to sit and feel the energy of the Gods pulsating through your body. Let any emotions you are experiencing rise to the surface. You may wish to dance, sing, etc. Embrace any feeling that comes to you. You might feel the need to go into a trance. Let the energy of the Gods take over you and awaken the divine within yourself. This may manifest through shaking or vibrating your body or ecstatically dancing.

When you feel it is time to end the rite, sit in a relaxing posture and slow your breathing. Focus on your breath and centre your energy. When ready, raise your wand and say:

> *"God and Goddess, Lord and Lady, the Old Gods. This rite is now complete. I am in you, you are in me. We are one. So mote it be."*

You can now close the circle.

The Offering Ceremony

Giving offerings to the Gods is a form of giving them thanks for what they provide. Through their vital energy, which is the earth's life force, our crops and food are grown. Making an offering returns this vital force to the God and Goddess, who in turn reciprocate this by returning the energy to us in the form of another cycle of crop and vegetation growth. Our lives are sustained through the consumption of the earth's food. Offering, therefore, continually circulates energy between the God and Goddess, the earth and all things that grow and eat from it. Thus, offerings emphasise the importance of reciprocity.

In Wiccacraft, offerings are made in the form of drinks and food. Drinks can be alcohol, such as cider, beer, mead, wine or fruit juice if you do not drink alcohol. In Ancient Greece, food offerings to Demeter, Goddess of the harvest and the earth's fertility, were made in the form of fruit. You can use fruit such as apples, pears, strawberries, blueberries, blackberries, pomegranates and grapes or grains such as wheat and barley for food offerings. The Offering Ceremony can be performed and incorporated into any Wiccacraftian ritual. It can also be performed as a ceremony in its own right.

To begin the ceremony, place the fruit or grains you wish to offer in a bowl or on a plate. Put this and the bottle of alcohol or fruit juice on the altar or the floor in front of the altar. Cast the circle. Open the bottle and pour some of the beverage into the altar chalice. Raise the chalice and say:

"God and Goddess, Lord and Lady, the Old Gods. I am here to give thanks for all the blessings of the earth that sustain us. I hold in my hand the nectar of the earth. I offer you this so that together we may celebrate the vitality of the divine. To the Gods."

Pour half of the drink into the offering bowl. Drink the rest. Take up the fruit or grains from the plate. Hold them in your hands, saying:

"Great God and Goddess. I hold in my hands the fruit of the earth, the body of the divine. I give thanks to you, the Old Gods of earth, air, fire and water, who make life and growth possible. I offer you the fruit that emerged from your divinity. Through this offering, we maintain our connection in the cycle of life, death and rebirth. To the Gods."

If the fruit is an apple or pear, cut off a piece and place it in the offering bowl. If you are offering berries or grapes, place one berry or grape in the offering bowl. If you are offering grains, place a few handfuls in the offering bowl. Eat the remainder of the fruit. You can consume the remaining grains after the ceremony.

You can reflect on how nature provides for us. You can think about how we are involved in a cycle of a reciprocal relationship with the God and Goddess and why it is important for us to be grateful for what the earth provides for us. When you feel ready, you can close the circle.

The drink and fruit should remain in the offering bowl overnight. The following day they should be returned to the earth. If you have a garden, you can tip the contents out onto the earth. If you do not have a garden or a compost heap, then you will have to dispose of the offerings in a different responsible way.

Return the bowl to the altar once the offering has been given back to the earth.

House Cleansing

A house cleansing should be performed to cleanse your home of its past and to make it your own space. It will turn your home into a spiritual sanctuary in which the God and Goddess are present. You should perform this ritual only once you have undergone the First Initiation and regularly connected with and prayed to the God and Goddess. You do not need to cast a circle for this ritual.

To start, light the Deity candles on the altar. Say the following words:

> *"God and Goddess, Lord and Lady, the Old Gods. I call to you to bear witness to this ritual. I ask you to be with me as I perform a cleansing of my home. Bless this home and make it a space of happiness, love, fulfilment and safety. I ask you to cleanse and protect my home and to forever be present in this space. So mote it be."*

Take some salt and mix it with the water in the water bowl, saying:

> *"May the life force of the salt join with the life force of the water and cleanse and bless everything they come into contact with."*

Light the incense. Take up the salt water and sprinkle it through the perimeter of the room you are in, ensuring that it comes into contact with every corner. In addition to the perimeter, sprinkle it anywhere in the room you intuitively feel needs to be cleansed. As you do this, feel the presence of the God and Goddess within you. Visualise them blessing the room and cleansing it of anything you want to remove. You can let the visualisation come naturally or you can visualise a white light spreading throughout the room from the sprinkles of salt water.

Once you have finished cleansing the room, repeat the same process in every room in the rest of the home and the garden, if you have one. While performing the ritual, you can repeat a mantra of:

"God and Goddess, Lord and Lady cleanse and bless this home."

You do not have to use this exact mantra. You may wish to use other words or you may want not to speak at all. Do what feels right for you.

Once you have finished sprinkling the salt water throughout your home, return to the altar and replace the salt bowl.

Take up the censer. In a similar manner as you used the salt water, take the burning incense throughout the room's perimeter, ensuring that the smoke reaches every corner. Repeat the same process throughout the home, visualising the white

House Cleansing

light and blessings of the God and Goddess filling the home. Return to the altar and set the censer down.

Now take up the anointing oil. Go to the window of the room you are currently in. Pour/rub some anointing oil onto your index finger (right or left) and draw a pentagram on the top beam of the windowsill. Do this above every window in the room, visualising the pentagram as white light. Now go to the door of the room. Pour/rub more anointing oil onto your finger and draw a pentagram on top of the door, visualising it as white light. Now move into the rest of the home and repeat the same process above every door and window. Using anointing oil like this is a form of protection at each room's entrances and symbolises the presence of the God and Goddess throughout the home. Return to the altar and replace the anointing oil. Say:

> *"God and Goddess, Lord and Lady, the Old Gods. This home has now been cleansed and filled with your presence. I ask you to forever watch over this dwelling, to protect it, to bless it and to make it a space of love, happiness and divinity. So mote it be."*

You can now blow out the Deity candles. The cleansing is complete.

Moon Ritual

The moon symbolises magic, tranquillity and wisdom. The powers of the moon can be drawn upon to gain insight, direct energy during magical rituals and to bring a sense of calm. In Greek mythology, the Witch Medea prayed to Hecate, the Goddess of Witchcraft and the spirit realm to help draw down the powers of the moon Goddess Selene. The Greek Goddesses Hecate, Artemis and Selene were often seen as a Triple Goddess of the moon, Witchcraft, the dead, forests, hunting and animals. The Romans viewed the Roman Goddess Diana as being an amalgamation of these three Greek Goddesses. These are the Goddesses whose power we draw upon during moon rituals.

Moon rituals should be performed once a month. Ideally, they should be performed during the full moon, but you can perform them during other phases of the moon if need be. If you want, you can use selenite in this ritual by holding it in your hands while you visualise and feel the energy of the Goddess in and around you. You can also wear a moon pendant or have ornaments or jewellery on the altar symbolising the moon, such as the triple moon. Once you have experience performing the Moon Ritual, you can incorporate elements of the invocation and evocation techniques discussed later on.

To start the Moon Ritual, light the three Deity candles and incense. Cast the circle. Sit cross-legged facing the altar and say:

"I call to you great Goddess of the moon and light, Goddess of spirits, Witchcraft and forests. Surround me in your mystical light so we may be one. So mote it be."

If using selenite, hold it in your hands and visualise and feel it drawing down the energy of the moon into your body. Take slow, deep breaths and feel the cool energy of the Goddess around you. Visualise her presence as moonlight that surrounds you and becomes one with you. Let any feelings or sensations you are experiencing come to the surface and flow through your body. Once you feel the presence and oneness of the Goddess, speak any words that come to you. If you want to, you can also say:

"I am Hecate, Artemis, Selene and Diana. I am known by many other names. I am Queen of Witchcraft, Lady of the forests and night. I am the divinity of the moon. I live within all Witches and it is from both within and without you will find me, as we are one. If it harms none, do what you will. I bring blessings and magical insight. Acts of love and pleasure are my domain. Witches alive and dead walk with me. We are eternal. We are one."

MOON RITUAL

Take some time to feel the calming and mystical presence of the Goddess. This is also an excellent time to perform magic and direct energy to manifest your goals. When you feel ready, you can end the ritual by closing the circle.

The Gods and Goddesses

Anglo-Saxon and Norse Pantheon

Frey/Ing

Frey, also known as Ing, is the God of fertility, regenerative energy, the earth's life force and all that grows from it, peace and prosperity. His symbols include the sun, rain, ships and horses. His sister is the Goddess Freya.

One of his main centres of worship was the Temple at Uppsala in Sweden (Ellis-Davidson 1990) and his priests were described as unmanly. The male followers of Frey are another example of how Pagan religious/spiritual specialists do not fit within the confines of heteronormative gender norms. Ellis-Davidson (1990) has argued that the male followers of Frey took part in a spiritual rite that involved marriage to the God.

Frey can be called to manifest or maintain peace, to focus your energies into working towards achieving your goals, to help you bring stability into your life if it is in disarray and to attract love. He is the God of satiety and feeling content and comfortable in your life.

Hymn to Frey

"I call to Frey, God of the rain and sun that sustains the earth, bringer of fulfillment and happiness. May you bring peace and harmony to my life and awaken the productive energies within myself as you do with the plants of the earth. Bless me with love and comfort. Surround me with your warmth. So mote it be."

Freya

Freya is the Goddess of *Seiðr*/Witchcraft/mediumship, battle and love. Her symbols are cats, falcons, shields and necklaces. One of her modes of travel was in a carriage pulled by cats.

In Norse mythology, she possessed a necklace known as *Brisingamen*, which may have been made of amber and she had the ability to fly by shifting into the shape of a bird (Ellis Davidson 1990). She was a significant Goddess for Norse and Anglo-Saxon Witches, who would evoke/invoke her and learn through her through mediumship and intuition.

Summon Freya for insight into divination, to improve your intuition, to connect with the divine through invocation and evocation, to experience spiritual flight and to further unleash your spiritual abilities as a Witch.

The Gods and Goddesses

Hymn to Freya

"Freya, Goddess of divination and mediumship, open the way for me to connect to the spirit realm, so I may receive guidance and wisdom from the Gods and Witches who came before me. May we travel together through the night sky in rapturous flight. Enhance my intuition and spiritual awareness as I embody my true path of Witchcraft. So mote it be."

Frigg

Frigg is the supreme mother Goddess in the Anglo-Saxon/Norse pantheon. Friday is named after her. She is a Goddess of home, childbirth and fate.

Hilda Ellis-Davidson (1990) states that women invoked her during labour. As a Goddess of fate, her role is to help her followers become fully realised individuals who follow their true calling. Fate in this context is not one you have no control over. Instead, fate is a state of equilibrium, living as who you are and living a fulfilling life as you were meant to. Certain circumstances can cause us to become disconnected from our fate. One of the aims of divination is to diagnose why this has happened and look for solutions to bring the individual back to a state of serenity and fulfilment.

Call on Frigg to help you follow your true path, bring things into your life that cause fulfilment and happiness and maintain a healthy home environment.

Hymn to Frigg

"I summon you, Frigg, Goddess of fate and security. Open the way for me to stay on my true path, to fully embrace who I am and to express my authentic self. Let nothing stray me away from the path of manifesting the divinity within me. So mote it be."

Woden/Odin

Woden/Odin, the All-Father, is a progenitor God of divination, mediumship, divine ecstasy, the dead and Witchcraft/*Seiðr*. His symbols were ravens and wolves. He is associated with the night and the colour black. Horned figures of Woden/Odin have been found in England, indicating that he was one of many horned Gods of Europe. Wednesday is named after him.

In the *Havamal* of the *Poetic Edda*, he describes how he hung from a tree and sacrificed himself to gain divine wisdom, which he did by taking up the runes (Ellis-Davidson 1990; Lindow 2001). This event signifies the spiritual death and rebirth that a Witch undergoes through initiation. It is a theme found among all cultures that believe that Gods and spirits can call people to become diviners and mediums. Lindow (2001) claims that the tree Odin hung from was Yggdrasil, the "World Tree", which

The Gods and Goddesses

is the universe in its entirety. Therefore, Odin also represents the spiritual interconnectedness of all things in existence and that a spiritual death and rebirth signify becoming one with this divine totality.

Prior to being referred to as Woden in Old English and Odin in Old Norse, he was named Wodan by the early Germanic people. Hilda Ellis-Davidson (1990) states that the Germanic sky God Tiwaz was merged with Wodan into one God (Odin) by the Norse people. Tiwaz is cognate with the Greek Zeus and Roman Jupiter and all three were a single God named Dyeus by the Proto-Indo-European people (Mallory and Adams 2006). Odin is referred to as Tyr in certain Old Norse texts (Ellis-Davidson 1990). I posit that they were the same God in Proto-Germanic times but referred to by different names. This makes sense in that Odin is the main God of the Norse pantheon. The majority of father-Gods in European Pagan religions are variations of the Proto-Indo-European God Dyeus.

Woden/Odin was frequently associated with divine ecstasy, madness and fury, which would occur when he was invoked or evoked by Witches (*Volur/Vitkar* in Old Norse). In the poem *Voluspa* in the *Poetic Edda*, he travels to the Underworld to consult a dead *Volva*, reflecting his association with both Witchcraft and the realm of the dead. He was

Lord of the Wild Hunt, a rite in which he flew through the night sky with spirits. Witchcraft/*Seiðr* in Norse regions of the world was usually associated with women and gay men. Odin, who was the God of *Seiðr*, is therefore also the God of the gender-nonconforming diviner. The specialists of divination and mediumship in most cultures do not conform to heteronormative ideas of gender. This can be explained by the fact that Witchcraft and its various forms/names are focused on the individual giving into their feelings and intuition to connect to the divine. They are therefore not restricted by artificially constructed gender norms. Thus Woden/Odin, Lord of Witchcraft, is also a God of homosexuality and gender-nonconformity.

Woden/Odin can be called upon to induce spiritual ecstasy, improve divination skills, gain divine insight, increase the potency of runic magic and facilitate spiritual death and rebirth (initiation) to become one with the divine energy that permeates the universe.

Hymn to Woden/Odin

> *"Woden, Lord of Witchcraft and night, I call on you to bless me with your sacred wisdom, so that I may understand the secrets of the runes. Let me be overcome with your divine ecstasy, so that I become one with the World Tree that connects all things. Woden, the essence of Witchcraft, I am one with you. So mote it be."*

Greek Pantheon

Artemis

Artemis is the Goddess of forests, mountains, animals, hunting and the untamed wilderness. Her symbols are deer and the bow and arrow. She is a virgin Goddess, a Goddess of solitude and hermits. Artemis is a Triple Goddess with the Goddess of Witchcraft Hecate and the Goddess of the moon, Selene.

In *Geography* by Strabo (1923), it is said that her sacred realm in the mountains and forests is a place where wild animals become tame, with humans being able to touch wolves and deer if they are in her domain. She was a protector of women during childbirth and was invoked by women in labour for this purpose (Aeschylus 1927). In the *Second Orphic Hymn*, she is described as a keeper of "Great Nature's Key" (Orpheus 1896:9).

Call on Artemis for wisdom and self-reflection. Feel her presence when you walk in forests or on the mountain. Channel her for independence and self-fulfilment. Ask her to bring calm and self-love in times of stress.

Hymn to Artemis

"I call to Artemis, the Goddess of the woods and mountains, the wild Goddess of the wilderness, she who lives in solitude. I ask for strength,

fulfilment and independence. May I be surrounded by the power of your sacred groves and gain wisdom through reflection in times of solitude. So mote it be."

Demeter

Demeter is the Goddess of the earth's fertility and the harvest. Her symbols are wheat and other grains, fruit and the plough.

She is frequently mentioned in the works of Hesiod as a Goddess of the earth and agriculture. She is particularly associated with grains and in the *Second Orphic Hymn* (Orpheus 1896) she is described as the giver of grain and a Goddess of joy.

Her association with the harvest also connected her with feelings of fulfilment. She was considered a vital Goddess, as the lives of people depended on her vitality to grow crops.

Call on Demeter to bring fulfilment into your life and accomplish goals that will be meaningful and rewarding. Work with her vital energy to create and be productive so that you will see satisfying results.

Hymn to Demeter

"Demeter, life force of the earth, hear my call. I ask that you bless me with success in all areas of

my life and that I will be rewarded for the hard work I undertake. May I have a future that is bountiful with everything that fulfils me. So mote it be."

Dionysus

Dionysus, also known as Bacchus, is the God of spiritual ecstasy, divine madness, frenzy, repetitive trance-inducing drumming, freedom, grapes, grapevines, wine, myrrh, *Goeteia*, *Manteia*, death and rebirth. He is also one of the main Greek Gods associated with homosexuality and gender-nonconformity. His symbols are grapevines, grapes, ivy, the colour purple, bulls, leopards, snakes and the thyrsus, which is a staff made of fennel covered in ivy leaves and topped with a pinecone.

His presence would cause plants to grow and surround things with ivy and grapevines. He is sometimes depicted as a horned God with the horns of a bull. In the *Orphic Hymn to Dionysus*, he is referred to as "Two horn'd, with ivy crown'd" (Orpheus 1896:68). His followers were known as Bacchae and Maenads and the rites that invoked him were called Dionysia and Bacchanalia. He is the God of destroying social constructions and unleashing the spirit within you. His followers were often described as being ecstatic, hysterical and frenzied when invoking him.

His male lover was Ampelus, who was killed by the moon Goddess Selene. Dionysus was grief-stricken after this event. He asked the Gods of the Underworld to bring his lover back and sensing his intense sadness, the Fate Atropos resurrected Ampelus in the form of a grapevine. Dionysus admired the beauty of his lover in his new form. Thus, he drank the juice of the grapevine and adorned himself with its leaves and tendrils. He became overcome with ecstasy and would travel the world liberating people from the bonds of their minds (Nonnus 1940).

In some traditions, Dionysus was divinely conceived and was begot from a virgin birth, as his mother Semele became pregnant after eating the heart of the first incarnation of Dionysus, who had been killed by a group of Titans (Pseudo-Hyginus 1960). Semele herself was killed by lightning while pregnant and Zeus took the infant and sewed him into his thigh until he was ready to be born (Pseudo-Hyginus 1960; Nonnus 1940). Dionysus is, therefore, a God of death and rebirth, as he was reborn after his death. As a God of resurrection, he could bring animals back from the dead and brought his mother back to life from the Underworld (Oppian 1928; Apollodorus 1921; Pausanias 1918).

Dionysus should be summoned to release your mind from the socially constructed norms that suppress us. Through a spiritual death and rebirth, he will unleash your true self through the destruction of the ego and enable you to fully manifest the divine within you, so that you can fully be in your power. Dionysus can be invoked/evoked to enter a state of ecstatic trance dancing, where you are overcome with the energy and forces of nature that permeate the earth. Through working with him, you can become one with the spirit of forests and all things that grow from the earth.

Hymn to Dionysus

"Horned God of the vine and ecstasy, liberator of the soul, roaring God of spirit dancing, I call to you. Free my mind and spirit from the constraints and socially constructed illusions of society. Let my true self emerge in all its glory. I dance with you and the Bacchae, Lord of resurrection. Deeper we go into a state of trance where we move with the spirits of trees and the vine. So mote it be".

Hecate

Hecate is the Goddess of Witchcraft/*Goeteia*, spirits of the dead, the Underworld and night. Her symbols are snakes, the moon, torches, the colours saffron and black and dogs. She is a Triple Goddess as Hecate-Artemis-Selene and she is, therefore, a Goddess of Witchcraft, the moon and forests.

She was one of the Titans, the Gods that came before the Olympian Gods. In addition to being the Goddess of the Underworld, the Ancient Greek poet Hesiod (1914) wrote that she was highly honoured by Zeus and other Gods, which resulted in her being given a place as a Goddess of the earth, sea and heavens. Because of the vast range of forces she symbolised, she was prayed to in order to grant a bountiful harvest, prosperity and good luck. However, she is primarily the Goddess of Witchcraft/*Goeteia* and the spiritual realm.

She is described as carrying a torch in the *Homeric Hymn to Demeter* when she helps Demeter look for her daughter Persephone in the Underworld. The Ancient Greek poet Bacchylides (1927) also referred to her as carrying a torch and being the daughter of Nyx, the Goddess of night. In the *First Orphic Hymn*, she is described as having an entourage of ghosts (Taylor 1792). In the epic tale of *Argonautica* (Jason and the Argonauts), written in the 3rd century BCE by Apollonius Rhodius (1912), she is a night-wanderer of the Underworld and Queen of the Dead. When summoned, she was adorned with snakes, coiling themselves around oak branches and she was surrounded by thousands of torches and barking dogs (Apollonius Rhodius 1912).

The Gods and Goddesses

In *Metamorphoses* by Ovid (1922), the Witch Medea channels the powers of the moon Goddess Selene through Hecate for her magic. The God Dionysus also calls out to Selene in *Dionysiacai* by Nonnus (1940) and calls her Hecate, who is known by many names. Hecate is mentioned numerous times in Ancient Greek and Roman literature as a Goddess of Witchcraft, the dead, the Underworld, the night and the moon. She is the personification of Witchcraft itself.

Call on Hecate when you are seeking to gain more wisdom and mystical experiences in your Wiccacraftian practice. Her energy will unleash the potency of Witchcraft from within yourself and she can be invoked/evoked for divination, magic, harnessing the power of the moon and connecting to the spirit realm.

Hymn to Hecate

> *"Hecate, the essence of Witchcraft, Goddess of the Underworld, esoteric wisdom and night, I call to you. She who is adorned with beautiful serpents and hounds of the Underworld. I, a Witch, come before you. Unleash the potent divinity within me, draw down the power of the moon into my body and connect me with the Witches who came before me and their sacred wisdom. So mote it be".*

Persephone

Persephone was Goddess of the Underworld, the dead, the changing seasons and death and rebirth. Her symbols include the pomegranate and the apple.

Plato (1793) viewed her as a Goddess of wisdom. She was the daughter of the earth Goddess Demeter. She was taken to the Underworld by Hades, where she remained for six months of the year, namely the dark half of the year. When in the Underworld, she is the Queen of the dead. With her return to the surface of the earth, she brought fertility to the earth and caused the vegetation that sustains us to grow. Prayers were made to her for peace, the growth of crops, health and harmony (Orpheus 1896). Her worshippers would ask her to grant them a place in her realm of the Underworld when they died (Orpheus 1896). She was a Goddess of death and rebirth by having both the ability to resurrect the dead in physical form (Pindar 1915; Plato 1925) and by welcoming the souls of the recently deceased into their new life in her realm (Pindar 1915).

In the *Odyssey* by Homer (1919), the Witch Circe tells Odysseus to travel to the Underworld and ask Persephone for permission to consult with the spirit of the prophet Teiresias. During this journey, Persephone sends him the souls of various dead women and warriors of old (Homer 1919).

Channel Persephone to connect with the spirits of the dead, improve your skills in mediumship and divination and engender change and shifts within yourself, as she is the Goddess of changing seasons and new beginnings. Working with her can help you start new chapters in your life.

Hymn to Persephone

"Persephone, Queen of the Underworld, Maiden of death and resurrection, I summon you. Reveal to me the wisdom of the dead Witches of old. May the change of the seasons you bring cause growth and learning within me, so I may be a fully realised Witch on a path of ever-growing strength and happiness. So mote it be".

Selene

Selene is the Goddess of the moon, magic, peace and tranquillity. Her symbols include the moon, including the Triple Goddess moon, horses and torches. In the *Ninth Orphic Hymn*, she is described as being a horned Goddess of silver light, who wonders the night (Orpheus 1896). She is extensively referenced in Ancient Greek writing, especially regarding the calm and beauty her light brings. The Witches Medea and Circe were said to have drawn down the power of Selene during their magical rites (Ovid 1922).

Call on Selene to bring calm, tranquillity and to enhance your divination techniques, for she elucidates that which is shrouded in darkness.

Hymn to Selene

"I call to the moon, Selene, Goddess of silver light. I draw down your calming energy, so my life may be full of peace and tranquillity. Surround me with your cold light and reveal to me the wisdom the darkness holds. So mote it be."

Celtic Pantheon

Brigid

Brigid was an earth Goddess associated with the first signs of spring, the fertility of the earth, new beginnings and good luck. Her symbols are the Brigid cross, hay, oats and other grains and snakes. Rituals and ceremonies that honoured her celebrated the renewal of the spring (Olmsted 2019).

Call on Brigid to ask for prosperity, fulfilment and success in the future.

Hymn to Brigid

"Brigid, Goddess of good fortune and renewal. Grant me blessings in the months ahead. May you

aid me in ensuring that the fruits of my labour are rewarded. So mote it be."

The Dagda

The Dagda is an All-Father progenitor sky God who was worshipped in Ireland. He was a God of magic, death and resurrection. His symbols are the staff, bones and musical instruments.

He had a club that he both killed and resurrected with (Olmsted 2019). He was strongly connected to magic and divine wisdom.

Call on the Dagda to improve your skills in magical practices and to let go of the past to make way for new beginnings.

Hymn to the Dagda

"I call to the Dagda, Lord of magic and resurrection. I ask for your aid in improving my magical knowledge and potency of my spells. Grant me your mystical wisdom, so the way is opened for me to fully manifest my magical potential. So mote it be."

Lugh

Lugh is the God of craftsmanship, creativity, art and the sun. His symbols are horses, horseshoes, hammers, apples, pears, grain and the sun.

The Pagan festival of Lughnasa is named after him, which is the first harvest festival. He was seen as a protector of vegetation and grain due to his association with crops (Olmsted 2019).

Call on Lugh to inspire creativity and assist you with completing creative projects in which you are involved.

Hymn to Lugh

> *"I call to the God of the first harvest, Lugh, the great smith. Bright God of the sun, bring out the creative forces within me so I may achieve my creative goals. So mote it be."*

The Eight Seasonal Festivals

The eight seasonal festivals celebrate the changes and cycles that the earth undergoes throughout the year. They honour the journey of the God and Goddess as they transform and embody different Deities according to the season. Through celebrating these festivals, Witches give thanks to the earth and all the forces of nature in a continual state of life, death and rebirth. These natural cycles provide for us, generating and circulating vital divine energy that causes life, such as plants and animals, to grow and survive. This energy is transferred back into the earth after a person dies when they become one with it and contribute to the regenerative stage of this cycle. Therefore, celebrating the seasonal festival makes us aware of the interconnectedness of everything in nature, on our journey in life, death and rebirth in the forces of nature.

These festivals were celebrated all over Pagan Europe, but in Gardnerian Wicca, they have been adapted from four Anglo-Saxon/Norse festivals and four Celtic festivals. Wiccacraft also celebrates these festivals, connecting them to specific Gods. The Anglo-Saxon/Norse festivals are Yule (Winter Solstice), Ostara (Spring Equinox), Midsummer/Litha (Summer Solstice) and Harvest

(Autumn Equinox). The four Celtic festivals are Imbolc, Beltane, Lughnasa and Samhain, which fall between the solstices and equinoxes.

All seasonal festivals should incorporate the Offering Ceremony into their performance. Offer food and drink that is appropriate for the specific festival. The altar should be decorated in foliage and symbols that are associated with the celebration of each festival. You can perform magic and divination during these ceremonies. If you use magic, the spell you perform should be connected to the symbolism of the festival you are celebrating. Festivals such as Ostara symbolise rebirth/new beginnings, while Midsummer would be an excellent ceremony for performing magic focused on bringing you confidence and mental and emotional strength.

The following entries on the festivals include verses that can be used to pray, invoke or evoke and honour the Gods associated with each festival and symbols connected to the specific celebration. As I have mentioned above, you should perform the Offering Ceremony for each ceremony and adapt it to the festival you are celebrating.

Yule

Northern Hemisphere: 21st-22nd of December

Southern Hemisphere: 20th-21st of June

Yule is the celebration of the Winter Solstice. It is the shortest day of the year and it marks the point from which the days will get longer. Yule was a major festival for the Norse people, who gave bountiful offerings to the Gods during this period. It is a festival of reciprocity, whereby we give thanks to the Gods and each other for all that they have blessed us with. In pre-Christian Pagan times, gift-giving maintained social relationships, both between humans and the Gods. Through giving offerings (gifts) to the Gods, we return to them what they have given to us and they will, in turn, return it to us again. This reciprocity specifically refers to the process whereby the Gods provide for us in the form of the earth and everything that grows from it that we consume and use to build and create. This productive divine energy is returned to the Gods, who re-circulate it to the earth and us. Yule is a time of family, friendship and hearty celebration. It is a time to strengthen social relationships and reflect on the meaningful people in our lives.

Yule is strongly associated with the God Woden, the All-Father, who in mythology and folklore flew through the night sky with his reindeer and wolves. This event was known as the "Wild Hunt".

Symbols of Yule include holly, ivy, pine trees, pinecones, cinnamon, reindeer and gifts.

Yule Hymn

"God of the night sky and flight, the All-Father who has been known by many names. I am here to give thanks for all the blessings you have bestowed upon me and I, in turn, gift you what you have gifted to me, for we are tied together in a sacred reciprocal bond. I ask you to strengthen my relationships and to surround me with love. So mote it be."

Imbolc

Northern Hemisphere: 1st-2nd of February

Southern Hemisphere: 1st-2nd of August

Imbolc marks the point in the year that signifies the very early signs of spring. It lies halfway between the Winter Solstice and Spring Equinox. The weather is still cold during this period, but the days have become longer and the light half of the year is emerging. It is a Celtic festival honouring the Goddess Brigid, a mother Goddess of healing and fertility (Ellis 1992).

This time of year also marks the return of the Goddess Persephone from the Underworld to the surface of the earth for the six lighter months of the year. It is a time to ask the Gods for a prosperous, peaceful and pleasant year. This is a good time to use divination to see what the year ahead holds for us.

Using divination during Imbolc can help the Witch see possible outcomes of the coming months and the methods that they can use to change the outcomes to be more favourable. This method of divination is discussed in the chapter on runes. Ceremonies can also be performed near rivers during this time, as rivers symbolise the Underworld and the dead, the realm from which Persephone is returning.

Symbols associated with Imbolc are Brigid's Cross, rushes, hay, oats, wheat, lilies, rivers and water.

Imbolc Hymn

> *"Goddess of early spring, I welcome your return. Brigid and Persephone, the plants awaken with your light and divinity. I ask for your wisdom for the year ahead. Cleanse and bless me with your light so I will be ready to manifest my goals and ambitions, powered by the divinity of you within me. Give me insight through divination of the coming months and the actions I can take to ensure I have a fruitful year. So mote it be."*

Ostara

Northern Hemisphere: 20th-21st of March

Southern Hemisphere: 22nd-23rd of September

Ostara was the Anglo-Saxon festival of the Goddess of dawn, Eostre/Ostara. It is a festival of new beginnings and rebirth. It is the Spring Equinox, where the day and night are of equal length. Ostara is a time to focus on your goals and start new projects. It is also a time of personal rebirth. Therefore you can use this time to practise rituals that help shift your mental state into a more encouraging and hopeful frame of mind where you focus on all the exciting possibilities of the future. You can do this by prayer to the God and Goddess, where you ask them to open the way for you to achieve all that you want to achieve and have a happy and fulfilling year ahead. You can also perform herbal and runic magic to concentrate your efforts on these goals.

Symbols of Ostara are rabbits, hares, decorative eggs, daffodils, tulips and irises.

Ostara Hymn

> *"I call to you, great Goddess of the dawn, she who wears flowers and nurtures new life. Ostara, Lady of rebirth and new beginnings, may you bless me with a happy and successful year ahead. I am asking you to nurture my personal and spiritual*

The Eight Seasonal Festivals

growth so that I can achieve all I want to accomplish. I let go of past worries and stresses so I may begin anew for a hopeful and fulfilling future. So mote it be."

Beltane/May Day

Northern Hemisphere: 1st of May

Southern Hemisphere: 1st of November

Beltane is a Celtic fire and fertility festival. It is the midpoint between the Spring Equinox and Summer Solstice. It is a festival of love and passion, making it a good time to perform rituals that aim to attract a lover for single people. For people who are married or partnered, it is a time to celebrate your relationship and love for each other. It is also a time to be grateful for your relationships and proud of the fruits of your labour and your achievements.

During Beltane celebrations, people believed that the smoke and ashes of the fire had protective qualities. Ash can be incorporated into your ritual as a form of protection of all that is dear to you. An example would be tracing the shape of the rune of protection, Algiz ᛉ, on your body with ash. You can also substitute the ash with your anointing oil. Beltane is a time to focus on maintaining all the things in your life that make you happy and the work that is involved in doing that.

Symbols of Beltane include fire (which can be represented as a red candle), ash, hawthorn and elks.

Beltane Hymn

"God and Goddess of fire, life and love, I come before you to celebrate the festival of passion, protection and gratitude. May the love I have for those who are dear to me be strengthened and kept. I ask you to protect the blessings I have received and everything I hold sacred. Let the divine smoke and ashes do their magical work by guarding all good fortune I have received. So mote it be."

Midsummer/Litha

Northern Hemisphere: 20th-21st of June

Southern Hemisphere: 21st-22nd of December

Midsummer takes place during the Summer Solstice, the longest day of the year and it has been celebrated throughout Europe. It is also the day that marks the beginning of the days becoming shorter. The Summer Solstice represents the Greek Goddess Demeter in her most potent form, as she is a fertility Goddess who brings light and the growth of crops for six months of the year.

Maypoles are erected in some European countries during Midsummer, which celebrants dance around. The maypole could have originally signified the World Tree Yggdrasil in Norse mythology, which represented the universe. Midsummer is a time of celebration, ecstatic dancing and reflecting on the interconnectedness of the natural world. It is also a time to think about your accomplishments and what you are proud of achieving. It is the festival of realised goals and fulfilment.

Symbols associated with Midsummer are the sun, ash trees, bonfires, wheat and snakes.

Midsummer Hymn

> *"I call to you, Goddess of life and growth. Demeter, I thank you for the regenerative power you bring and the light with which you surround me. I come before you to honour your manifestation in me, which is reflected in my accomplishments and realised goals. We are one. You are the force within me that drives me to generate and create. I am one with the World Tree, which connects all beings in the natural world. May I forever be aware of the divinity that unites us. So mote it be."*

Lughnasa/Lammas

Northern Hemisphere: 1st of August

Southern Hemisphere: 1st of February

Lughnasa is the festival of the Celtic God Lugh, a Deity of the sun, creativity and craftmanship (Ellis 1992). The festival was called Lammas by the Anglo-Saxons. It occurs at the midpoint between the Summer Solstice and Autumn Equinox. It is the first harvest festival, when Witches celebrate the fruition of the first crops and give thanks to the earth and sun Deities, who sustain our life.

Lughnasa is also a time to draw on the Gods for creative inspiration. If you are working on a creative project such as a work of art, a book, jewellery design or metalworking, you can perform magic to try and enhance and strongly manifest that creative part of yourself.

Symbols associated with Lughnasa are items made from metal such as jewellery, apples, any items you use to create art and fruit such as apples and pears.

Lughnasa Hymn

"God of the sun, generator of life, grower of crops. I honour you for continuing to provide the fruits of the earth. Bless our future harvests so they may be bountiful and satiating. Lugh, God of artists and smiths, I ask for your divine inspiration so that my

creativity flows through me into my art and work. Awaken and unleash the creative energies from within me so that my art embodies the innovative forces of my spirit. So mote it be."

Harvest

Northern Hemisphere: 22nd-23rd of September

Southern Hemisphere: 20th-21st of March

The Harvest festival falls on the Autumn Equinox. It is a time to celebrate and have feasts made from the bountiful crops that have been harvested during this time. It is a good festival for performing ecstatic dancing and it is associated with the God Dionysus. While this is a time to celebrate, it is also a time to prepare for the cold months ahead so that harmony can remain in the home and community. The harvested crops are there to be enjoyed during the festivities. Still, they are simultaneously respected and the participants in the festivities should remain conscious that the fruits of their labour will need to last for the coming months.

Symbols associated with Harvest include apples, pears, wheat, barley, oats and other grains.

Harvest Hymn

"Great God of the harvest, I call to you to join in the celebration of this year's fruits and grains, for which I give thanks. Dionysus, let your ecstatic energy surround me and unleash the electrifying energy in my body. May my spirit dance and celebrate during this time of joy. I feel you flow through my veins, a divine frenzy that brings ecstasy. I am one with you. So mote it be."

Samhain

Northern Hemisphere: 31st of October

Southern Hemisphere: 30th of April

Samhain was the Celtic festival of honouring the dead. It was a time for the community to celebrate with and take part in a feast of the spirits of the deceased. Those who came before us are a part of us, for we are all descended from the same lifeforms that first emerged on this planet. Therefore, the spirits of the dead connect us to the beginning of time and through them, we can connect to everything in existence. Samhain is a good time to practise divination, as it is associated with the Deities of the spirit realm, who possess esoteric wisdom. Use Samhain as a time to honour all the Witches who came before you and to give thanks to them for their work and transmitted wisdom.

Symbols of Samhain include bones, water (in many cultures, spirits of the dead are associated with rivers and the ocean), the moon, turnips, beets, pumpkins and leaves that have fallen from trees.

Samhain Hymn

"I call to the God and Goddess of the spirit realm, who have been known as Persephone, Hecate, Woden and many other names. Through you, I give thanks to the dead and all the blessings they have bestowed upon us. I honour all the Witches who have come before me and the wisdom they have given us. I ask for their continued guidance, strength and protection. Great horned God of divination, give me insight into the magical workings of the runes and all they wish to communicate to us. Gods of the spirit realm and Witchcraft, we walk together as one. So mote it be."

The Second Initiation

The Second Initiation should be performed when you feel you have made significant progress in your Wiccacraftian practice. When you are ready to complete the Second Initiation, you should have experience casting the circle, the Offering Ceremony, performing moon rituals, celebrating at least one seasonal festival and praying regularly to the God and Goddess. You should feel more in touch with your intuition and have a strong connection to the God and Goddess. The time it will take you to get to this point will depend on the individual. It can be one month, a few months or a few years. It is essential that you feel ready for it and feel that it is the right time.

This initiation uses the *Nine Herbs Charm* and application of the herbs to your body. The *Nine Herbs Charm* is an Anglo-Saxon charm from the early Medieval period written in Old English. It was written down after the Christianisation of the Anglo-Saxons, but it is Pagan in origin. The medical text it is written in is the *Lacnunga*, in which the charm is specifically used to treat a physical ailment, but in the context of this rite, it will be used for the Second Initiation of a Witch.

The charm makes use of herbs that were most sacred to the All-Father and Witch God Woden/Odin and the Anglo-Saxons. After applying the herbs to your body, their energy will live within you and become one with your spirit, causing you to become closer to the God and Goddess. Witches would talk to herbs directly when performing magical herbal rites. The herbs were believed to be living entities that had their own distinct energy. The Witch would ask the herbs to perform their magic to be effective in the rituals in which they were used.

I have adapted the words of this charm from Oswald Cockayne's 1864 translation of the Anglo-Saxon medical text known as the *Lacnunga*, which was written in the tenth century in England. The name of the God Woden appears in the original charm, but I have added it in another section and I have also inserted the name of the God and Goddess in the appropriate part.

This initiation can be conducted while wearing clothing and your ritual sarong, but during the part that involves applying the sacred salve, you might wish to perform it in your underwear, as the mixture can get onto your clothing if you apply it while fully clad. If wearing clothing and underwear, it is necessary to wear clothes that allow you to apply the mixture to your body. If you perform the entire ceremony in your underwear, you should wear your ritual sarong for all of the steps until you get to the stage where you apply the salve to your body.

The Second Initiation

The herbs you will need for this initiation are betony/wood betony, mugwort/wormwood, chamomile, plantain leaf, nettle, lamb's lettuce (also known as corn salad), thyme and fennel. The herbs should be in dried form, but if you cannot obtain them in this form, you can use the seeds of the herbs. If you cannot find these herbs, then you can use similar herbs in the same family. You will also need an apple, apple juice, a bar of natural mint soap and ashes. If you cannot find natural mint soap, then use natural soap made with another herb that you associate with calmness. The tools you will need are a mortar and pestle, a pot and spoon for boiling and stirring the mixture, a knife to cut the apple and soap and a cauldron from which you will apply the sacred salve. This ritual can result in the mixture spilling onto the ground/floor, so it would also be helpful to have a piece of fabric or towel on the surface underneath you.

I have retained the original Old English names of the herbs in my adaptation of this charm's translation by Oswald Cockayne. The word "wort" was the Old English word for herbs, which is why they are referred to as "worts" in this incantation. Do not use these herbs if you are allergic to them or think you will have a bad reaction from using them. If this is the case, then find related herbs that will not cause an adverse reaction. Do not use fresh nettle, as it can sting. Only use nettle after it has been dried.

This initiation will take place while seated on the floor, facing your altar. Gather all your ingredients and tools and place them on the floor in front of you. The herbs should be placed on the floor in a straight line while still in their bags. Light the Deity candles, incense and cast the circle. Facing the altar, say:

"God and Goddess, Lord and Lady, the Old Gods. I call to you to bear witness to my second initiation into the path of Wiccacraft. Let your divine energy live within me through these sacred herbs of the Old Gods. May they bring me ever closer to you. So mote it be."

Focus your attention on the herbs. Feel the power emanating from them and recite the following over them three times:

"Have a mind, Mugwort,

What thou mentioned

What thou prepared

At the prime telling

Una though highest Eldest of worts

Thou hast might for three

The Second Initiation

And against thirty

For venom avails

For flying vile things

Mighty against loathed ones

That through the land rove

And thou, Waybread,

Mother of worts

Open from eastward,

Mighty within

Over thee carts creaked

Over thee queens rode

Over thee brides bridalled

Over thee bulls breathed

All these thou withstood

And with stunning noise stayed

As thou withstood

Venom and vile things

And all the loathly ones

That through the land rove

WICCACRAFT

Steem is called this wort,

On stone she grew

Standeth she against venom,

Stoundeth she head wark

Stiff she is called

Stoundeth she venom,

Wreaketh on the wrath one,

Whirleth out poison

This is the wort which

Fought against worm

This avails for venom

For flying vile things

Tis good against the loathly ones

That through the land rove

Flee now

Attorlothe

The less from the greater

The greater the less

Till boot from them both be

The Second Initiation

Have in mind, thou Maythen,

What thou mentioned

What thou accomplished

At Alderford

That never for flying ill

Fatally fell man

Since we to him Maythen

For medicine mixed up

This is the wort which is Called Wergule

This sent the seal

Over seas ridge

Of other mischief

The malice to mend

These nine can march on

Against nine ugly poisons

A worm sneaking came

To slay and to slaughter

Then took up Woden

Nine wondrous twigs

WICCACRAFT

He smote then the adder

Till it flew in nine bits.

There ended it the Crab Apple

And its venom, that never it

Should more in house come

Chervil and Fennel

Two fair and mighty ones,

These worts Woden formed

Wise he and witty is

Holy in heaven

Them he suspended

And sent to the seven worlds

For the poor and the rich

Panacea for all

It standeth against pain

It stoundeth at venom,

Strong it is against three

And against thirty

Against the hand of the fiend,

THE SECOND INITIATION

Against foul fascination

Of farm stock of mine

Now these nine worts avail

Against nine exiles from glory

Against nine venoms

And nine flying vile things,

Against the red venom

Against the stinking venom

Against the white venom

Against the watchet venom

Against the yellow venom

Against the green venom,

Against wan livid venom

Against the brown venom

Against the purple venom

Against worm blister

Against water blister

Against thorn blister

Against thistle blister

Against ice blister

Against poison blister

If any ill come flying from East

Or any come from North

Or any from West Over the human race

Woden stood over men opposingly

I alone know him beaming and the nine adders behold him

All weeds now may give way to worts

I become one with the God and Goddess

So mote it be."

It is now time to mix the herbs and apple. Take the eight herbs (one at a time) and place them in the mortar. You will need three pinches of each herb. Cut off a piece of the apple and place it in the mortar with the herbs.

Once all eight herbs and the apple have been placed in the mortar, start grinding them with the pestle. Grind them as fine as possible.

Now add the ash and apple juice. The amount of apple juice used is up to you, but a quarter of a cup is the maximum you should use.

The Second Initiation

Carry on grinding, ensuring that the herbs are well-mixed with the apple juice.

Take up the soap and cut three pieces off, adding them to the mixture. Grind the soap into the mixture. You can chant the following while grinding:

"These sacred herbs will become one with me and bring me closer to the God and Goddess."

Once you have a well-mixed concoction, pour all of the mixture into the pot. You will now need to leave the circle, by opening a circle door and go to the kitchen to boil the mixture.

Place the pot on the stove and set it to a high temperature. Take the spoon and stir the mixture continually. It will come to a boil and it should start frothing. Carry on stirring when it reaches boiling point. This will create a thick, foamy and concentrated salve.

Once you feel that the salve is concentrated enough, take the pot back to the circle. Carefully set the pot down on the mat and close the circle door you created once you return to the circle.

Sit with the mixture on the floor, facing the altar and pour it into your cauldron. Wait for it to cool down to a lukewarm temperature. Sense the power of the herbs emanating from the cauldron.

It is now time to apply the mixture to your body. You will do this using your fingers. Using your right or left hand, dip your index and middle fingers into the salve and lift some of it up. The ointment should be thick, so this should not be difficult.

Rub the salve on the centre of your scalp, visualising it as a white light that becomes one with you. Take more of the ointment and rub it on the centre of your forehead, continuing to visualise it as a white light. Apply the rest of the salve in the following order: the base of your neck, your chin, your shoulders, the centre of your chest, the top of your thighs, your pubic area, the outer sides of your knees and your ankles.

Take a while to sit and feel the power of the herbs. Feel their energy become a part of you. When you feel ready, turn your attention to the altar, saying:

"God and Goddess, Lord and Lady, the Old Gods. Through the sacred herbs of the Gods, you live within me. These herbs bless me, protect me and keep me close to you. I am in you, you are in me, we are one. So mote it be."

The Second Initiation is now complete. Take some time to feel the power of the herbs within your body. You can also perform the Offering Ceremony if you wish. Once you have finished, close the circle in the usual manner.

The Second Initiation

Do not wash the ointment off until the following day. You need to sleep with the salve on your body overnight. The remaining herbs that you did not use can be kept in your altar if you have space or in a separate area with your other magical items.

Invoking the Gods

Invocation is the ritual in which a Witch takes the Gods into themselves and becomes one with them. It was one of the most important rites in pre-Christian Pagan Witchcraft. Through invocation, Witches received sacred knowledge and wisdom and communicated it to the community and people consulting them. It was also important for the Witches themselves and it allowed them to experience the full manifestation of the Gods in their bodies. It could result in ecstasy, personal wisdom and a sensation of strength, empowerment and spiritual connectedness with the divine. This ritual should be started while sitting down. The literary, linguistic and archaeological evidence I discussed earlier indicate that Witches performed this rite while seated.

The Witch is fully responsible for what occurs during an invocation and it cannot be used as an excuse for irresponsible behaviour. Invocation leads to both the Gods and the Witch becoming one with each other. Therefore, the Witch is still in control of their actions while performing this rite.

The invocation ritual I have provided is an invocation of the Goddess. You can alter the words of the invocation according to which Deity you are choosing to invoke. I have provided hymns that can be used for various Deities in the chapter on Gods and Goddesses.

The Invocation Ritual

Light the three Deity candles on the altar and the incense. Cast the circle in the usual way. Sit cross-legged, facing the altar. When you are ready say:

"Great Goddess, Lady of all, Goddess of the moon and bringer of life. I call to you to become one with me. So mote it be."

Rest your hands on your knees with the palms facing upwards. Close your eyes and focus your attention on your breathing. Let your mind be completely blank, letting any thought gently melt away. Now visualise a white light entering your body from your head, with it moving down your spine and into all areas of your body. Start to rapidly move the base of your spine up and down, while seated, so that your entire torso is moving upwards and downwards. Feel the energy move throughout your body from your spine. Shake/vibrate your arms and hands. Continue to move the base of your spine up and down. You can also rock backwards and forwards if you want to. Let the vibration move throughout your body until your entire body is shaking/vibrating. Let the energy of the Goddess completely take over. You can stand up and dance if you want to, with the power transforming from shaking into high energy

Invoking the Gods

dancing or movement. You can remain seated if you wish, but continue to vibrate and shake your body, experiencing the Goddess. Continue to keep this high level of energy going. Let any feelings, emotions or sensations come to the surface. You can express these through speaking, singing, laughing or other means which come naturally to you in the moment. You may experience a feeling of divine ecstasy. While in this state of trance, messages might come to you in the form of images in your mind, such as colours or symbols of nature. If an image of the ocean comes to you, this might indicate travel or the need to perform a ceremony near the ocean or a ceremony at home involving water. If a colour comes to you, such as red or pink, this might indicate love is coming your way or that you are loved and surrounded by the love of the God and Goddess.

The symbols might be difficult to interpret, but once this rite is finished you can reflect on and write down what you experienced. If you want to you can write down the images or words coming to you while still in a state of trance, but if you do this, ensure you keep the high-level energy going. Do not overthink anything; let the words, emotions and images just come to you. You can also record the rite on your phone or a video camera.

If you wish to engage in magic or spell work during the invocation, do this once the energy of the

Goddess has completely taken over your body. You may want to attract something into your life, such as love. You can do this while in a trance by speaking as the Goddess, stating:

"I am the embodiment of love, thus love shall surround me and manifest in my life in the form of someone who loves and respects me for who I am."

Remember, both you and the Goddess have become one. Therefore you are speaking as a single entity. You might wish to visualise a colourful energy that represents love surrounding you and being close to you during this ritual. Do not focus on attracting the love of a specific person, as that goes against the Wiccan Rede. You can also drink alcohol or juice and eat fruit as an offering to the Goddess while she has manifested in you, but ensure you keep the energy flowing and moving.

Once you feel ready, it is time to bring the invocation to an end. Sit cross-legged, facing the altar. Close your eyes and focus on your breathing. Take slow deep breaths. Focus your attention on the centre of your body, with your energy feeling completely centred. Once you feel centred and calm, the invocation has come to an end. You may wish to write down what occurred while still in the circle or you can do this once the circle has been closed.

Invoking the Gods

Once you have completed everything you wanted to do, take up the wand, raise it and face the east. Announce:

> *"God and Goddess, Lord and Lady, the Old Gods. This invocation and these rites have now come to an end."*

You can now close the circle.

Evoking the Gods

Evocation is the ritual in which the Gods are summoned so that the Witch can deeply enter the spiritual realm. While all Wiccacraftian rituals involve calling on the Gods to be present, evocation consists of interacting with that energy in a way that enables us to experience spiritual flight or journeying through the spiritual realm. The Witch may experience insights and wisdom through thoughts, epiphanies, images and feelings during evocation. These can be written down during or after the evocation ritual, in the same way as the invocation ritual.

The following ritual is an evocation of the God. You can adapt the evocation words according to which Deity is being evoked. I have provided hymns for calling other Deities in the chapter on Gods and Goddesses.

The Evocation Ritual

Light the three Deity candles and the incense. If you have a crystal ball, made from amethyst or quartz, ensure that you can easily view it on the altar. Cast the circle. Sit cross-legged, facing the altar and say the following words:

"Horned God, Lord of night and King of the spirit realm. I call to you to be present and surround me

WICCACRAFT

with your divine light so that I may receive wisdom and insight. So mote it be."

Close your eyes and focus on your breathing. Let any thought that emerges dissolve so that your mind is like a blank canvas. Visualise the white light of the God surrounding you and the space you are in. Feel his presence. Open your eyes and focus on the crystal ball. If you do not have crystals, focus on a specific point in the room. Do this while breathing deeply and slowly, staying focused on the same area. After staring at the crystal ball or one area of the room for some time, you may see the energy of the God. This could be in the form of flowing white light or mist radiating from the area you are focusing on. If you do not see anything, then become aware of the God's presence by feeling it in the room. Feel as if you are part of this energy, with your body transforming into white light. You can interact with the energy of the God by dancing or moving with it, going deeper and deeper into the spiritual realm. You can visualise your spirit flying through the night sky, over forests or mountains or swimming in the ocean and the rivers or ascending through the heavens or travelling through the spirit realms. Let the sensations and experiences come to you, whether they be physical sensations or visuals.

EVOKING THE GODS

During this evocation ritual, you can also ask the God for blessings or to help you manifest that which you are seeking. If you are looking for insight or wisdom, ask the God to reveal these to you. Let any thoughts or images that come to you as a result of your request emerge. You can write these down while performing the evocation or when the rite is over. You do not have to stand up for this ritual. You can remain seated for its entire duration if you wish.

When you feel it is time to end the evocation, sit in a cross-legged position, facing the altar. Slow your breathing and feel your spirit centred in your body. Become aware of your physical body, paying attention to the feeling of your body on the floor and the feeling of your hands against your knees or thighs. Ensure that you feel fully grounded and centred before you formally end the ritual. Take as long as you need for this to happen. Once you are grounded, the ritual can come to an end. Take up your wand. Stand up and raise it, facing the altar. State:

"The Horned God, Lord of night, King of the spirit realm. I thank you for your presence and wisdom. This evocation is now brought to an end."

Close the circle when you feel ready to do so.

Runes

The runes are an ancient alphabet used by the Germanic peoples such as the Anglo-Saxons, Norsemen, Goths and Franks. The runes developed from the Italic alphabet, which was, in turn, descended from the Greek alphabet. The runes used in this book are known as the Elder Futhark. They are the oldest form of the Germanic runes, with the earliest recorded inscriptions dating from the 2nd century. They were used for writing and for magical purposes, such as creating charms, performing spells and divination. In Norse mythology, the God Woden/Odin underwent a spiritual death and rebirth, giving him esoteric wisdom and knowledge of the runes. The word rune means secret. This refers to the fact that they are used for divinatory purposes whereby the diviner can gain insights into the past, present and future by using them.

The following is a list of the Elder Futhark runes. I have used Ralph Elliott's (1959:49) Proto-Germanic spelling of the rune names and his translations of the rune names into English.

The Runes

ᚠ Fehu

Cattle - Indicates matters relating to money. In ancient times and the early Medieval period, cattle were seen as a form of wealth. Use this rune in magic that is aimed at improving your financial situation. Using Fehu as a charm can help give you the confidence to find ways to remedy any issues relating to money. You can consult the runes through divination to see where Fehu lies in relation to the rune Mannaz ᛗ, representing you. If Fehu is far away from ᛗ this could indicate financial issues. Look at the other runes surrounding ᛗ, to see which factors are blocking a stable financial situation. Think of ways to deal with these issues and cast the runes again to see if the changes you make will improve your situation. This method of runic divination can be applied to all the runes and this is discussed and explained in this chapter.

ᚢ Uruz

Aurochs (Ox) - Represents strength. Use this rune to build up your confidence or to help yourself get through challenging situations where you need to be resilient.

Þ Thurisaz

Giants/Thor - Symbol of the lightning God Thor and the giants of Norse mythology. It represents power and confidence. Use this rune to channel assertiveness, personal strength and tenacity. Thurisaz can be used for motivation and confidence in any projects on which you are working.

F Ansuz

The word for God - This rune is a term for the Gods in general, but it is also specifically associated with Woden/Odin. Use this rune to bring you closer to the Gods. It is a powerful rune to help you gain spiritual insight and increase the potency of your magic and your divination skills.

R Raido

Riding/Journey - In divination, this rune signifies travel, change and inner spiritual journeys exploring the divine. Use this rune if you want to make changes in your life and to help you attract new experiences that will increase your spiritual knowledge.

ᚲ Kaunaz

Torch - Indicates light, knowledge and revelation. Use this rune to gain knowledge, insight and solutions to things you are unsure of, such as decision-making. The aim of using this rune is to help you think more clearly about the options you have when making decisions. It is, therefore, a rune of clarity and of knowing.

ᚷ Gebo

Gift - Represents offerings to the Gods and reciprocal relationships between humans and the Gods.

ᚹ Wunjo

Joy - The rune of happiness. Use it to nurture feelings of joy within. Visualise all the things that bring you joy when working with this rune and visualise the future as one where you will be happy and fulfilled.

ᚺ Hagalaz

Hail - Hail represents destruction. If this rune falls near Mannaz ᛗ, it indicates that there could be instability in your life. Analyse the runes that have fallen around Hagalaz to see what factors could be causing this instability. The rune can also represent letting go of the past and new beginnings. Use this rune in magic if you want a drastic shift in your life and want to let go of the things that are not conducive to your well-being.

ᚾ Naudiz

Need - This rune represents stressful situations and challenges that will result in learning, wisdom and fulfilment if they are overcome. Naudiz can signify to the Witch that they are on their correct journey and the rune is associated with fate. It indicates that you are learning challenging lessons but will emerge from them wiser. For example, you could be working on a project that you find difficult and stressful but want to come to fruition and have a result that you are proud of. It is the rune of perseverance and tenacity. Use this rune to give yourself the strength to continue on your journey to succeed in your endeavours.

ᛁ Isa

Ice - Represents calmness and serenity. It can also represent being stuck in a stagnant situation and not moving forward in your life. When using divination, the Witch needs to interpret which of these two traits the rune is signifying at that moment. If the Witch is feeling overworked and stressed and the Isa rune falls far away from Mannaz ᛗ, this indicates that they could channel the energies of the Isa rune to slow down the frantic pace of their life.

ᛃ Jera

Year - Represents the harvest and the fruits of your labour. Use this rune to attract blessings for the future, such as good fortune, friendship, love, success in work and projects and personal satisfaction. In divination, it signifies good luck and blessings from the God and Goddess. It indicates that your projects have been or will be successful.

ᛇ Eiwaz

Yew Tree - Represents strength and strong foundations. This rune signifies stability within your life. Use it to set down roots and to build a life you find fulfilling and secure. In divination, it indicates whether your life currently does or does not have solid foundations and security, depending on where it falls.

ᛈ Perth

Pear or fruit tree - Symbolises friendship, joy, happiness and conviviality. Use this rune to attract friends who will make you happy, have fun experiences and have a joyful life.

ᛦ Algiz

Elk - Represents protection and defence. Use this rune to give you strength and protection from anything in your life that is causing you distress. Algiz could be used to channel your assertiveness and not let the perceptions of others affect you.

ᛋ Sowulo

Sun - You can use this rune to channel the life-giving and productive energy of the sun. Use it to increase motivation and to be effective in your work. In divination it symbolises vitality and vigour.

ᛏ Teiwaz

The God Tiwaz - Tiwaz was a major Deity among the early Germanic people. He is the Germanic equivalent of the Greek God Zeus and the Roman God Jupiter, with all three Gods being known as "Sky Fathers" (Mallory and Adams 2006:409). All three of these Gods originally had the Proto Indo-European name Dyeus (Mallory and Adams 2006). The God Tiwaz was probably one form of the God Woden/Odin, who also has the epithet of "Father God". Like Ansuz ᚨ, you can use this rune to call on the power of the Gods and keep them close to you. The Sky Father Gods this rune represents are powerful Deities and therefore you can use this rune to channel strength, protection, vitality and spiritual potency. If this rune falls near to Mannaz ᛗ, it indicates that you are in a strong position of personal power and harmony in your life.

ᛒ Berkana

Birch Twig - Birch symbolises cleansing and new beginnings. You can channel its energy in preparation for initiation rites. In divination, Birch signifies change or starting a new chapter in your life.

ᛗ Ehwaz

Horse - The horse was sacred to the ancient Germanic peoples and associated with the sun (Elliott 1959). This rune is therefore associated with warmth and comfort. You can use it to manifest feelings of relaxation and kindness to yourself.

ᛗ Mannaz

Man - Mannaz represents the person consulting the runes during divination. The position of all the other runes in relation to Mannaz is analysed to determine what the runes are communicating to us about the person's present situation and future and what activities can be performed to change the outcome of the future.

ᛚ Laguz

Water - This rune symbolises the spirit world. It can be used to connect with your forebearers, whether they be biological ancestors, Witches who came before you or other historical figures with whom you feel a connection. If the rune falls near Mannaz ᛗ, it indicates that the spirits of the departed are protecting and guiding you.

ᛝ Ingwaz

The God Ing - Ing was another name of the fertility God Frey. The rune symbolises creativity, productive energy and the growth and nurturing of goals.

ᛟ Othila

Property, land and inheritance - This rune relates to matters around your home, land or property you want to buy or property you will inherit. In divination, it can reflect which factors are influencing your home life. It can also symbolise buying or inheriting property. Use this rune in magic that focuses on opening the way for you to buy property or use it to ask for harmony in your home life.

ᛞ Dagaz

Day - Dagaz symbolises clarity. Use it to find the answers you are seeking and to increase your wisdom. If it falls near Mannaz ᛗ, it indicates Dagaz will reveal the answers you are looking for soon.

Divination with Runes

The runes are associated with hidden divine knowledge. Divination is how the Witch gains insight into the past, present and future possibilities. Witches can use divination to determine what is currently going on in their life and it can provide solutions to issues that they are experiencing. When consulting the runes about the future, they can present outcomes that reflect what will occur if the Witch continues with their current activities without making any changes. This predicted outcome could either be favourable or unfavourable. If the outcome is favourable, the Witch can continue with their activities as usual. If the runes present a future outcome that the Witch is not happy with, they can consult the runes again to ask what actions they can take to change the future outcome to a more favourable one. To change a predicted outcome, the runes might indicate that the Witch needs to perform a specific ritual or change their current life situation.

You can use runes for divination by throwing them on the ground, also known as casting lots. You can do this by keeping the runes in a pouch that is emptied onto the floor. The way the runes fall can be read to assess the situation of the person consulting them.

You do not need to cast the circle when reading runes, but you should light the three Deity candles and the incense so that you can call on the Gods of divination. Deities closely associated with divination are Woden/Odin, Freya and Hecate.

To start the divination session, light the three Deity candles and incense. Sit facing the altar with the rune pouch in your hands. Say:

"I call on the Gods of the runes, Deities of divination and sacred wisdom. Give me insight into the nature of the runes, so I may interpret the messages they convey to me. So mote it be."

Open the pouch and blow into it once. Shake the pouch gently and repetitively. Ask your question as you do this. This can be verbally or in your mind. If you want a general reading of what your current situation is, say:

WICCACRAFT

"I ask the Gods to show me insight into my current life."

Repeat this phrase as you shake the runes in their pouch. When you feel it is time, empty the pouch of runes onto the ground. Turn up all the runes that have fallen face down. The first rune you need to look for is Mannaz ᛗ. This rune represents you. Look at where all the other runes have fallen in relation to ᛗ. The runes closest to ᛗ represent the forces that are currently affecting your life. For example, if the rune Thurisaz ᚦ lies close to ᛗ, this could indicate that you are in a place of strength and power. In a different reading, the rune Ansuz ᚠ, representing the Gods, could fall far away from ᛗ. This could indicate that you need to focus more on your Wiccacraftian practice to feel fulfilled and connected to the Gods. You could remedy this by performing the Offering Ceremony. To see if this will be effective, place all the runes back into the pouch. Start shaking them as before and ask:

"Will my situation improve if I make an offering to the Gods?"

Repeat this as you shake the pouch of runes. When ready, empty the pouch onto the floor. If the rune Ansuz ᚠ is now closer to ᛗ, this indicates that an offering will work in bringing you blessings and maintaining your relationship with the Gods. You might also find that runes representing joy ᚹ

and fertility ᚠ now lie closer to ᛗ. If ᚠ still lies far away from ᛗ, you can think of other ways to remedy the situation and cast the runes again to see what particular course of action will work.

Runic Spell

You can use the runes for your spiritual development and they can assist you in realising your goals. They can help you channel the energies associated with the goal you want to achieve, whether it be to form friendships with people you connect with, find love or attract good fortune and maintain stability in your life. You can use them to nurture feelings within yourself, such as confidence, fulfilment and happiness. The following runic spell can be adapted to use the specific rune appropriate for what you hope to achieve.

This spell aims to awaken happiness and joy within yourself and to attract things in your life that will bring you joy and happiness. You can use it if you have been experiencing a low mood, whether short-term or long-term. This spell is not meant to be a cure; it is used to assist you with your mental health journey by shifting your focus onto the emotional state you want to embody. The rune used in this ritual is Wunjo ᚹ, meaning joy.

For this ritual, you will need your anointing oil, in addition to your regular magical tools. Light the

Deity candles and the incense. Cast the circle. Sit facing the altar and hold the anointing oil in your hands. Say:

"I call to the Gods of the runes, masters of sacred knowledge and divination. I call on the power of Wunjo, the rune of joy. I ask you to bring me happiness, fulfilment and stability. Fill my life with things that bring me joy and pleasure. May this rune be one with my body through this holy oil. So mote it be."

Open the bottle of anointing oil. Cover your index finger in the oil and draw the shape ᚹ on the centre of your scalp. As you draw the rune, visualise it as a bright white light. Draw the rune on your forehead, the base of your neck, your chin, your shoulders, the centre of your chest, the top of your thighs, your pubic area, the outer sides of your knees and your ankles. Place the anointing oil on the altar. Close your eyes and feel the power of the rune, bringing you feelings of joy, warmth and comfort. Visualise the power and joy of the rune moving through your body until it engulfs your whole being. When you feel ready, raise your wand and say:

"I am one with Wunjo, the rune of joy. All will be well. So mote it be."

You can now end the ritual by closing the circle.

Runic Charm

You can create a runic charm to intensify your focus on what you want to achieve or attract in your life. You can create a charm that you carry with you daily, such as in your pocket or bag or you may wish to hang the charm in your bedroom so that you are visually and subconsciously aware of the rune and what it represents. Carrying the rune or displaying it in your bedroom will cause shifts within your psyche, which will assist you in achieving the intended outcome of using it.

If you are going to create a charm, you can engrave the rune on a small piece of wood or paint it on a stone or any other object that will be easy enough to carry around. You can also draw the rune on a piece of paper, which you can fold up so it easily fits into your pocket or bag. If you are going to use a drawing of a rune to hang up in your bedroom, you can use a simple blank page of paper and draw it using a pencil, pen or marker. Runes are usually written in black, red or white. If you draw the rune in white, you will need a black piece of paper and a marker or pen with white ink. It would be best if you drew the rune in the centre of the page. You can also draw and create patterns, doodles, lines and symbols around the rune. Draw anything that you feel the rune is naturally bringing out of you. You might find that other symbols come to you while drawing.

WICCACRAFT

The following ritual will use the rune ◊, called Ingwaz, representing the God Frey, God of fertility and growth. This ritual focuses on achieving your goals on a personal project and making your ideas come to fruition. This can be a creative project you are working on, such as a painting, writing a book, sewing a garment, writing a dissertation or a business project in the workplace. Using the Ingwaz ◊ rune will help you concentrate your focus on the creative process and its end goal.

To start the ritual, gather all the items you will need and place them on the ground, facing the altar. Light the three Deity candles and the incense. Cast the circle. When you are ready, say:

"I call to the ancient Gods of the runes, Gods of divine knowledge and wisdom. I call upon the power of Ingwaz, rune of fertility, growth, creativity and realised goals. I ask you to be with me and surround me with your power, so that my creative projects and work are successful. So mote it be."

Now you can start engraving or drawing your rune. While creating an image of the rune, think of the project you are working on. If you are working on a dissertation, visualise yourself writing it with confidence. Envision both the process of writing and the end goal being successful and something you are proud of. Continue to visualise this process and feel the creative and productive energy emanating from the rune once you have finished engraving or drawing it.

When you feel ready, end the ritual by saying:

"Ingwaz, you bring me creativity, productivity and success. Help me to realise my goals. You are with me. So mote it be."

You can now close the circle.

If you have created a charm to carry with you, carry it with you throughout the day. When you go to sleep, place it next to your bed on a bedside table or somewhere close to you if you do not have a bedside table, such as under your pillow. If you have created a drawing, hang it up on your bedroom wall. If this is not possible, try resting it against the wall on a piece of furniture, such as a chest of drawers, wardrobe or bookcase. You should carry or display the rune until you have achieved your desired outcome or for a longer period of time. After the rune has done its work, you can display it on your altar or store it with your other ritual items. If you have created a drawing or painting of the rune, you can keep it in a bookbinder file, which you can also use to keep other rune drawings or paintings you do in the future.

Herbal Magic

In Wiccacraft, herbs/plants/trees are used primarily for their spiritual effects rather than for their physical effects. It is what they represent spiritually and symbolically that matters. While most herbs do cause a physiological response, this is not the primary reason for their use in Witchcraft. In pre-Christian Pagan times, there was a distinction between specialists who used herbs to heal physical conditions and specialists such as Witches, who used herbs for spiritual matters.

You can use herbs for a variety of things. Witches can utilise them to connect to the God and Goddess or a specific Deity. They can be used to bring good luck or to help you move on from past experiences so you can feel cleansed and fresh for new beginnings. You can bathe in herbs, use them to create magical oils, mix them in your cauldron and leave them on your altar, mix them into a paste or liquid and apply them to your body, burn them, sleep with them under your pillow or carry them around in a pouch. The method you choose should be based on what you intuitively feel is right.

Witches should use herbs in their dried or essential oil form. Do not use any herbs that you are allergic to, have had adverse reactions to in the past or that you think you will have a bad reaction to.

Herbs and other plants that can be used in magical practice

Ash - The World Tree, wisdom, intuition and divination.

Betony/Wood Betony - Initiation, connection with the Gods, divination, invocation, evocation, knowledge and protection. One of the most sacred herbs of the Anglo-Saxons.

Blackberry leaf - Happiness, contentment and motivation.

Chervil - Wisdom and knowledge.

Chamomile - Peace, relaxation and safety.

Common Sage/European Sage - Summoning the Gods, cleansing and consecrating.

Clover - Good luck, security, harmony and tranquillity.

Croton - Growth, manifesting ideas and projects, focusing your thoughts to achieve your goals, creativity and productivity.

Cypress - The Goddess Hecate, divination, invocation, evocation and the spirit realm.

Fennel - Cleansing and protection.

Frankincense - Initiation, consecration and summoning the Gods.

Ivy - Knowledge, intuition and wisdom.

Jasmine - Creating a sacred space, rites of passage, initiation, consecration, connection with the Gods and intuition.

Lamb's Lettuce/Corn Flower - Motivation, energy and vitality.

Lavender - Relaxation, intuition, peace and satiety.

Mint - The Goddesses Persephone, Demeter and Hecate, the spirit realm, invocation, evocation, tranquillity, relaxation, cleansing, blessings and new beginnings.

Mugwort/Wormwood - Summoning the Gods, entering the spirit realm, spiritual flight, invocation and evocation and divine wisdom. It is associated with the Goddesses Hecate, Artemis, Selene, Diana and the God Woden/Odin.

Myrrh - The Gods Hecate, Dionysus, Persephone and Woden, the spirit realm, initiation, consecration, invocation and evocation.

Nettle - Creativity and the strength and motivation to achieve your goals.

Oak - Divination, wisdom, intuition

Plantain - Confidence, emotional strength and assertiveness.

Periwinkle - Protection.

Rose - Happiness, fulfilment, good luck and realised goals.

Rosemary - Cleansing and connecting with the spirit realm.

Sea Holly - Good luck, friendship and happiness.

Thyme - Courage, bravery and assertiveness.

Herbal Charm

You can carry around a charm using herbs with you to draw on its energies to achieve your desired outcome. The following ritual is an example of using betony to keep the Gods close to you during difficult times where you feel you need to call on their love, strength and protection.

For this ritual, you will need dried betony, which can be purchased from various places. You will also need a pouch that tightens at the top and that you can easily carry around with you. It should be big enough to hold three pinches of betony.

To start the ritual, place all of the ingredients and tools needed on the altar or floor in front of you, so that they will be within the circle. Light the incense and deity candles. Cast the circle. Once this is done, sit with the herbs in front of you. Say:

"I call to the Gods of this sacred herb betony. Awaken its power so that it may keep me close to you. I ask for this herb to remind me of your love and protection for me. So mote it be."

Turn your attention to the betony, saying:

"Betony, divine wort of the Old Gods. Be with me so I continually feel the love and protection of the God and Goddess. I ask you to assist in restoring harmony to my life. So mote it be."

Visualise a warm light emanating from the herb. Visualise this light rising from the herbs and around your body, bringing you feelings of love and protection. When ready, take three pinches of the betony and place them in the pouch. Seal the pouch and say:

"God and Goddess, Lord and Lady, the Old Gods. Through this charm of the sacred herb betony, I will be reminded of your love, protection and oneness with me. So mote it be."

You can now end the ritual by closing the circle. Carry the charm with you for however long you need to. Once you feel like it has achieved its purpose, store it with your other magical items so you can use it again in the future if need be.

Herbal Cauldron Magic

Another way of using herbs is to create a mixture using a cauldron. Placing the herbs in your cauldron on the altar for a period of time will build up the energy of the herbs. Your cauldron is tied to you energetically and therefore letting the herbs sit for a while will cause the power within yourself to shift and achieve your desired outcome. The cauldron represents the earth, as well as the void from which all creation sprang. Placing objects within it symbolises planting the seeds of your goals. The following ritual uses chamomile and mint to bring peace, relaxation and harmony. This ritual can be adapted to use other herbs for different desired outcomes.

For this ritual you will need a miniature cauldron on your altar, water, chamomile, mint and a spoon, preferably wooden or silver. Light the Deity candles and incense. Cast the circle. Address the God and Goddess saying:

> *"God and Goddess, Lord and Lady, the Old Gods. I come before you to create a herbal brew with mint and chamomile, to bring me calm and peace. I ask that you bless these herbs so they will restore quiet to my life. I ask you to be with me and guide me through the process of herbal-craft. So mote it be."*

Place the herbs in front of you, either on the altar or on the floor. Speak to the herbs directly, saying:

"Mint and Chamomile, I ask you to bless my life with peace, relaxation and harmony. So mote it be."

Once this is done, place the herbs into the mortar, grinding them until you feel they are ready. While doing this, stay focused on your goal. You may wish to chant or repeat prayers to the God and Goddess and the herbs. You can also think of all the things that bring calm and peace to your life while engaged in this process. Once you have finished, pour the water into the cauldron. Take the herbs and place them in the cauldron with your fingers. Stir the mixture together and say:

"May the magical ability of these herbs mix with the life giving force of the water so they will come together to manifest tranquillity in my life. I ask that serenity grows and brews within this cauldron, a symbol of the primordial waters and the earth. May the energy of this mixture surround me and be within me, so that I can find peace within myself and in my surroundings. So mote it be."

Now address the God and Goddess, stating:

"God and Goddess, Lord and Lady, the Old Gods. This rite is now brought to an end. May you

and the sacred herbs grant me what I desire. So mote it be."

You can now close the circle. Leave the brew on your altar for as long as you feel necessary. It would be best if you buried the mixture in your garden when you feel it has done its work, saying:

"To the Gods."

If you do not have a garden, then you should find another means of disposing of it responsibly.

Creating Magical Oil For Spell Work

A variety of magical oils can be created by combining the herbs listed earlier in this chapter with olive oil and the power of the runes. The combination of magical herbs with runic symbols can result in powerful spell work. The following spell uses mint essential oil mixed with olive oil and the rune Fehu ᚠ to manifest good luck. You can combine these ingredients to create a reusable oil for future spells or rituals relating to good luck or you can create a mixture to be used only once.

If you wish to create a reusable oil, you will need olive oil as a base oil, an empty vial and mint/garden mint essential oil. If you will only be using this oil for one spell, you will not need the vial, but you will need a small cauldron.

To start the spell, place the ingredients and tools needed on your altar. Light the incense, deity candles and cast the circle. Facing the altar, raise your wand and say:

"I call to the Gods of good luck, prosperity and the precious stones of the earth to be with me and work through me in the creation of a sacred oil to bring me good fortune. So mote it be."

If you are creating a reusable oil, open the empty vial and fill three quarters of it with the olive oil. Open the bottle of mint essential oil and pour fifteen drops into the vial while saying:

"May the oil of mint mix with the sacred olive oil and bring prosperity, good luck and blessings with all they come into contact with. So mote it be."

Seal the vial and hold it in your hands. Visualise the vial as being filled with a liquid of white light. Feel its cold energy in your hands. Once you have spent some time becoming aware of the feeling of the oil, state:

"Fehu, rune of good fortune, I ask you to imbue this oil with your essence so that it may manifest blessings in my life. So mote it be."

If you are creating an oil to only be used once, repeat the steps above, but pour the olive and mint oil into your cauldron instead of the vial.

Once the oil has been created, it is time to apply it to your body. Cover the tip of your index finger with the oil. draw the shape ᚠ on the centre of your scalp, while chanting:

"Fehu, Fehu, Fehu."

Feel the bright but cool energy of the oil entering and flowing through your body, bringing a sense of relaxation. Cover your index finger in the oil again and draw the rune on your forehead, the base of your neck, your chin, your shoulders, the centre of your chest, the top of your thighs, your pubic area, the outer sides of your knees and your ankles, continuing to chant:

"Fehu, Fehu, Fehu."

Use as much oil as necessary to trace the symbols over these areas of your body. Rub any remaining oil on your hands through your hair. Once you are done, sit facing the altar. Take a few moments to feel the power of the oil within you, become aware of its sensations and its energy. Visualise what you wish to attract into your life. When ready say:

"Gods of the earth, the source of good fortune and prosperity, your sacred essence lives within me; may it open the path for me to receive your blessings. So mote it be."

Close the circle when you feel ready. Wait until the following day to bathe or shower.

Keep the vial for use in future spells to bring good luck. If you want, cover the vial with a label with the ᚠ rune on it to reinforce its properties of good fortune. If you used a cauldron, dispose of the oil in a responsible way once the ritual is over.

The above method for creating magical oil can be adapted to create a variety of oils for spell work by using and mixing the various magical herbs listed earlier in this chapter, which each have their own purpose. A base oil, such as olive oil, should be used for all concoctions. You can also adapt the above spell by changing the rune used so that it aligns with the spell you are performing and its goals.

The Third Initiation

The Third Initiation is the final initiation into the path of Wiccacraft. This rite will affirm and solidify your oneness with the God and Goddess, the Lord and Lady and the Old Gods. It is the final stage of answering your calling as a Witch. It should be performed once you have experience in invocation, evocation, divination and all the rituals and ceremonies required for the Second Initiation. This final initiation should be performed when it feels right for you.

You will need a red drink for this ritual, such as red cider, red wine, red mead or cranberry juice if you do not drink alcohol. This represents the blood of the God and Goddess, their vital divine life force, which circulates through the earth, plants, animals and people. This energy connects and flows through everything in the universe. Through the Third Initiation, the Witch becomes one with this energy in its purest form.

The main tools that you will use for this initiation are the chalice and offering bowl.

Place the bottle of the drink you have chosen on the altar or the floor. Light the Deity candles and the incense. Cast the circle. Sit facing the altar, stating:

> *"God and Goddess, Lord and Lady, the Old Gods. I am here before you to perform my third and final initiation into the path of Wiccacraft, for my soul is that of a Witch."*

Take up the bottle of the drink and open it. Pour some of it into the chalice. Raise it, exclaiming:

> *"God and Goddess, Lord and Lady, the Old Gods. I hold your blood in this chalice, your divinity that permeates all things. I take all of you into me. So mote it be."*

Drink all of the beverage in the chalice. Feel the energy of the Gods inside you and all the sensations it brings. Pour more of the drink from the bottle into the chalice. Raise it, exclaiming:

> *"God and Goddess, Lord and Lady, the Old Gods. I hold in this cup my blood, my divine life force, which is one with your divinity. Through this blood, we are forever connected and forever one, for I am eternally a Witch. So mote it be."*

Pour the entire drink from the chalice into the offering bowl, saying:

> *"To the Gods."*

Pour the drink from the bottle into the chalice again. Raise it, saying:

> *"God and Goddess, Lord and Lady, the Old Gods. I hold in this chalice your blood and my*

The Third Initiation

blood as we are one. My soul will forever walk the path of Wiccacraft. My soul is that of a Witch, the Old Gods live in me and I live in them. God and Goddess, Lord and Lady, the Old Gods. We are one. I am in you, you are in me. So mote it be."

Pour half of the drink from the chalice into the offering bowl, saying:

"To the Gods."

Drink the remaining liquid in the chalice. The Third Initiation is now complete. Take some time to feel the Gods both in you and around you. Let any feelings or sensations you are feeling manifest themselves. Feel their energy flowing through you. You might feel ecstatic, strong or calm. Dance or sing if you want to, feeling the Gods both within you and surrounding you. When you feel ready, close the circle in the usual manner.

Conclusion

Through the teachings and practices presented in this book, you have been offered methods to answer your calling as a Witch. You have been given initiation rites to become one with the Old Gods and fully manifest your identity as a Witch. The path of Wiccacraft is the path of being your authentic self, of intuition and the senses. It is the path of the Pagan Witch, one who awakens the Gods within themselves and is eternally connected to the divine forces of nature that permeate the universe.

Bibliography

Adler, M. (2006). *Drawing Down the Moon: Witches, Druids, Goddess-Worshippers and Other Pagans in America.* London: Penguin Books.

Aelfric (1881). *Aelfric's Lives of Saints.* Translated by W.W. Skeat. London: N. Trubner and Co.

Aeschylus (1927). *Suppliant Maidens in: Aeschylus.* Volume 1. Translated by H.W. Smyth. Cambridge: Harvard University Press.

Allman, G.J. (1877). *Greek Geometry, from Thales to Euclid.* Dublin: Ponsonby and Murphy.

Apollodorus (1921). *The Library.* Volumes 1-2. Translated by J.G. Frazer. Cambridge: Harvard University Press.

Apollonius Rhodius (1912). *The Argonautica.* Translated by R.C. Seaton. Cambridge: Harvard University Press.

Aristotle (1922). *De Caelo.* Translated by J.L. Stocks. Oxford: Oxford University Press.

Attenborough, F.L. (1922). *The Laws of the Earliest English Kings.* Cambridge: Cambridge University Press.

Bacchylides (1927). *Lyra Graeca*. Volume 3. London: William Heinemann.

Bede (1990). *Ecclesiastical History of the English People*. London: Penguin.

Bray, O. (1908). *The Elder or Poetic Edda, Commonly Known as Sæmund's Edda*. London: Viking Club.

Buchanan, C.D. (1933). Substantivized Adjectives in Old Norse. *Language*, 9(2), pp. 5-58.

Buckland, R. (2004). *Wicca for One: The Path of Solitary Witchcraft*. New York: Citadel Press.

Burkert, W. (1985). *Greek Religion*. Harvard University Press.

Cameron, M.L. (1993). *Anglo-Saxon Medicine*. Cambridge: Cambridge University Press.

Carver, M., Sanmark, A. and Semple, S. (2010). *Signals of Belief in Early England: Anglo-Saxon Paganism Revisited*. Oxford: Oxbow Books.

Clayton, M. (2008). The Old English "Promissio Regis." *Anglo-Saxon England*, 37, pp. 91-150.

Cockayne, O. (1864). *Leechdoms, Wortcunning and Starcraft of Early England*. Volumes 1-3. London: Longman, Green and Roberts.

BIBLIOGRAPHY

Coimbra, F. (2008). The Pentagram in Rock Art: Some Interpretive Possibilities. In Coimbra, F.A. and Dubal, L. *Symbolism in Rock Art*, pp. 7-12. Oxford: Archaeopress.

Coimbra, F. (2011). The Symbolism of the Pentagram in West European Rock Art: A Semiotic Approach. In *XXIV Valcamonica Symposium Proceedings, Art and Communication in Preliterate Societies*, pp. 122-129. Capo di Ponte.

Coimbra, F.A. (2016). Symbols for Protection in War among European Societies (1000 BC - 1000 AD). In Coimbra, F., Delfino, D., Sirbu, V. and Schuster, C. eds. *Late Prehistory and Protohistory: Bronze Age and Iron Age*. Oxford: Archaeopress Publishing.

Collins, R. (1999). *Early Medieval Europe 300-1000*. Basingstoke: Macmillan Press Ltd.

Cornford, F.M. (1937). *Plato's Cosmology*. New York: Liberal Arts Press.

Crawford, J. (1963). Evidences for Witchcraft In Anglo-Saxon England. *Medium Ævum*, 32(2), pp. 99-116.

Crawford, J. (2015). *The Poetic Edda: Stories of the Norse Gods and Heroes*. Indianapolis: Hackett Publishing Company Inc.

Cunningham, S. (2017). *Wicca: A Guide for the Solitary Practitioner*. St. Paul: Llewellyn Publications.

Dickie, M. (2003). *Magic and Magicians in the Greco-Roman World*. London: Routledge.

DK (2020). *History of Magic, Witchcraft and the Occult*. London: Dorling Kindersley Publishing, Incorporated.

Elliott, R.W.V. (1959). *Runes: An Introduction*. Manchester: Manchester University Press.

Ellis, P.B. (1992). *Dictionary of Celtic Mythology*. Santa Barbara: ABC-CLIO.

Ellis-Davidson, H. (1988). *Myths and Symbols in Pagan Europe: Early Scandinavian and Celtic Religions*. Syracuse: Syracuse University Press.

Ellis-Davidson, H.R. (1990). *Gods and Myths of Northern Europe*. London: Penguin.

Euripides (2015). *The Bacchae*. Translated by I. Johnston. Oxford: Faenum Publishing.

Foster, M. C. (2010). *The Cultural Imaginary of Manteia*. University of California.

Gardner, G.B. (1970). *Witchcraft Today*. London: Arrow Books.

BIBLIOGRAPHY

Gardner, G.B. (2004). *The Meaning of Witchcraft*. York Beach: Red Wheel/Weiser.

Geoffrey of Monmouth (1966). *The History of the Kings of Britain*. London: Penguin.

Griffiths, B. (2012). *Aspects of Anglo-Saxon Magic*. Ely: Anglo-Saxon Books.

Hall, A. (2007). *Elves in Anglo-Saxon England: Matters of Belief, Health, Gender and Identity*. Boydell Press.

Hamerow, H., Hinton, D. A., & Crawford, S. (2011). *The Oxford Handbook of Anglo-Saxon Archaeology*. Oxford: Oxford University Press.

Heselton, P. (2012). *Witchfather: A Life of Gerald Gardner*. Volume 1-Into the Witch Cult. Loughborough: Thoth Publications.

Hesiod (1914). *Hesiod, the Homeric Hymns and Homerica*. Translated by H.G. Evelyn-White. London: Heinemann.

Holmes, G. (2001). *The Oxford History of Medieval Europe*. Oxford: Oxford University Press.

Homer (1919). *The Odyssey*. Volumes 1-2. Translated by A.T. Murray. Cambridge: Harvard University Press.

Hyginus (1960). *The Myths of Hyginus*. Translated by M. Grant. Lawrence: University of Kansas Press.

Johnston, S. (2008). Magic and the Dead in Classical Greece. In: J.C.B. Petropoulos, ed. *Greek Magic: Ancient, Medieval and Modern*, pp. 14-20. Abingdon: Routledge.

Jolly, K. L. (1996). *Popular Religion in Late Saxon England: Elf Charms in Context*. University of North Carolina Press.

Koch, J.T. ed. (2006). *Celtic Culture: A Historical Encyclopedia*. Volume 2. Santa Barbara: ABC-Clio.

Levada, M. and Looijenga, T. (2019). A Recently Found Belt Buckle with Rune-Like Signs from Ukraine. *Journal of Archaeology and Ancient History*, 25. pp.1-18.

Liberman, A. (2008). *An Analytic Dictionary of English Etymology: An Introduction*. Minneapolis: University of Minnesota Press.

Lindow, J. (2002). *Norse Mythology: A Guide to the Gods, Heroes, Rituals and Beliefs*. Oxford: Oxford University Press.

Liuzza, R.M. (2001). Anglo-Saxon Prognostics in Context: A Survey and Handlist of Manuscripts. *Anglo-Saxon England*, 30, pp.181-230.

BIBLIOGRAPHY

Luck, G. (2006). *Arcana Mundi: Magic and the Occult in the Greek and Roman Worlds.* Baltimore: The Johns Hopkins University Press.

Mallory, J.P. and Adams, D.Q. (2006). *The Oxford Introduction to Proto-Indo-European and the Proto-Indo-European World.* Oxford: Oxford University Press.

Meaney, A. (1981). *Anglo-Saxon Amulets and Curing Stones.* British Archaeological Reports.

Meaney, A. L. (2004). "And we forbeodað eornostlice ælcne hæðenscipe": Wulfstan and Late Anglo-Saxon and Norse 'Heathenism'. In: M. Townend, ed. *Wulfstan, Archbishop of York: The Proceedings of the Second Alcuin Conference*, pp. 461-500. Turnhout: Brepols.

Mitchell, S. A. (2011). *Witchcraft and Magic in the Nordic Middle Ages.* Philadelphia: University of Pennsylvania Press.

Murray, M.A. (1921). *The Witch-Cult in Western Europe.* Oxford: Clarendon Press.

Nonnus of Panopolis (1940). *Dionysiaca.* Volumes 1-3. Translated by W.H.D. Rouse. Cambridge: Harvard University Press.

Ohlgren, T.H. (1988). The Pagan Iconography of Christian Ideas: Tree-lore in Anglo-Viking England. *Mediaevistik*, 1, pp. 145-173.

Olmsted, G. (2019). *The Gods of the Celts and the Indo-Europeans.* Tazewell: Garett Olmsted.

Oppian (1928). Cynegetica. In *Oppian, Colluthus, Tryphiodorus.* Translated by A.W. Mair. London: William Heinemann.

Orchard, A. (1998). *Dictionary of Norse Myth and Legend.* London: Cassell.

Orpheus (1896). *The Mystical Hymns of Orpheus.* Translated by T. Taylor. London: Bertram Dobell.

Ovid (1922). *Metamorphoses.* Translated by B. More. Boston: Cornhill.

Page, R.I. (1999). *An Introduction to English Runes.* Woodbridge: The Boydell Press.

Pausanias (1918). *Description of Greece.* Translated by W.H.S. Jones and H.A. Ormerod. London: William Heinemann.

Pindar (1915). *The Odes of Pindar Including the Principal Fragments.* Translated by J. Sandys. London: William Heinemann.

Plato. (1793). *The Cratylus, Phædo, Parmenides and Timæus.* Translated by T. Taylor. London: Benjamin and John White.

BIBLIOGRAPHY

Plato (1925). *Lysis. Symposium.* Gorgias. Translated by W.R.M. Lamb. Cambridge: Harvard University Press.

Plato (1929). *Plato: Timaeus and Critias.* Translated by A.E. Taylor. London: Methuen and Co. Limited.

Pollington, S. (2008). *Leechcraft: Early English charms, Plant Lore and Healing.* Ely: Anglo-Saxon Books.

Pollington, S. (2011). *The Elder Gods: The Otherworld of Early England.* Ely: Anglo-Saxon Books.

Price, N.S. (2002). *The Viking Way: Religion and War in Late Iron Age Scandinavia.* Uppsala: Deptartment of Archaeology and Ancient History.

Price, N. (2004). *The Archaeology of Seiðr: Circumpolar Traditions in Viking Pre-Christian Religion.* Brathair.

Serjeantson, M.S. (1936). The Vocabulary of Folklore in Old and Middle English. *Folklore*, 47(1), pp. 42-73.

Solli, B. (2008). Queering the Cosmology of the Vikings: A Queer Analysis of the Cult of Odin and "Holy White Stones." *Journal of Homosexuality*, 54(1-2), pp.192-208.

Stenton, F.M. (2001). *Anglo-Saxon England.* Oxford: Oxford University Press.

Strabo (1923). Geography. In *The Geography of Strabo.* Volumes 1-2. Translated by H.L. Jones. London: William Heinemann.

Strömbäck, D. (1975). *Sejd: Textstudier i nordisk religionshistoria.* Stockholm: Nordiska Museet.

Sturtevant, A.M. (1927). Some Etymologies of Certain Old Words Dealing with the Supernatural. *Scandinavian Studies and Notes,* 9(5), pp. 151-159.

Sturtevant, A.M. (1952). Comments on Three Proper Names in the Elder Edda. *Scandinavian Studies,* 25(3), pp. 100-102.

Uzdavinys, A. (2004). *The Golden Chain: An Anthology of Pythagorean and Platonic Philosophy.* Bloomington: World Wisdom.

Wood, F.A. (1914). Germanic Etymologies. *Modern Philology,* 11(3), pp. 315-338.

About The Author

Liam Peter Keene has been practising Pagan Witchcraft since the year 2000. He studied Religious Studies and Social Anthropology at university, focusing on Paganism, Ancient Near Eastern Religions, Hinduism, Shamanism and Traditional African Religion. He lives in Norwich, Norfolk, in the East of England.

www.ingramcontent.com/pod-product-compliance
Lightning Source LLC
Chambersburg PA
CBHW071457040426
42444CB00008B/1388